Dividend Investing

An Easy Guide for Beginners to Financial Freedom in the Stock Market by Making Money Using Passive Income.
Simple Investment Strategies Allowing You to Quickly Create Wealth.

Brandon Scott

1

Table of Contents

Introduction

Many investors continue to seek income generating investments in this uncertain environment. While most people tend to think of savings accounts, bank CDs, and bonds when your bring up the term "income investing", the most lucrative way to earn income from your investments in today's environment is the stock market.

And that is unlikely to change. Central banks have an almost knee jerk reaction when it comes to mild economic difficulties – they cut interest rates. This makes it harder to earn income from bonds or financial instruments from banks. In fact, in Europe interest rates are now slightly negative, which means that if you put your money into a savings account, you would/could actually lose money. But this is true even with small positive interest rates like banks pay in the United States. Interest rates are so low that they fail to keep up with inflation.

Even financial instruments that used to be a practically guaranteed way to grow capital are no longer worth it. Bank CDs pay rates around 3%, barely exceeding or keeping up with inflation.

While bonds offer some security for your capital, they are also paying dismal rates, unless you seek out bonds from entities or corporations that have bad credit. But who wants to risk their capital with a company that might not return your principal, for a halfway decent interest rate? Quite frankly that does not represent a good tradeoff for your investment capital. This all sounds dismal, but there is a better way, and we're going to talk about how you can earn a solid income with a historically proven, and relatively safe method. This is by investing in stocks that pay dividends. Overall, if you are not doing something that carries inherent risk like investing in penny stocks, stocks that pay dividends are low risk investments.

Companies do not pay dividends until they have matured, which means that these are companies that weather major economic storms and often come out stronger. Any solid stock that you invest in that pays good dividends is going to be one that survived the 2008 financial crisis, the 2001 dot com bust, and many even survived the Great Depression.

Dividend investing is as old as stock markets themselves, and this offers you a solid opportunity to build up wealth not only from dividend payments but also from the appreciation of the shares that you invest in.

The greatest investors of our time like Warren Buffett agree, investing in dividend stocks is a solid way to secure your financial independence. In this book we will explain dividend investing from the perspective of educating the beginning investor. So, no prior knowledge of stock markets or dividend investing is assumed. We will explain what it is, how it works, and how to go about your investing. We will also explore different options for investing that you may not have been aware of. You are probably anxious to get started, so, let us get going!

Please note that this book is for informational and educational purposes only. It is not meant to be taken as financial advice. You should consult a professional financial advisor if you need financial advice for your own investments. Any disclosures of income from stocks or other investments in this book is for information only. Past performance is not a guarantee of future returns.

Chapter 1: What Are Dividend Stocks

In this chapter we are going to teach you about dividend stocks from the ground up. No prior knowledge is assumed. We will briefly cover how the stock market works and what dividend payments are. We will also reveal why some stocks pay dividends and some stocks do not, and how to find the stocks that reliably pay good dividends. We'll also review the concept of compound interest, which is central to the way dividends work. But since stocks themselves appreciate in value, compound interest is far more powerful for investors than savings accounts or other vehicles are. It is like compound interest on steroids.

Overview of the Stock Market

Bear with me as I give a general description of the stock market for those readers who are complete beginners, to make sure that everyone understands what investing in stocks is all about.

Stock markets came into existence in the 17th century, as part of the age of exploration in Europe. At that time, people were building large sea vessels to "explore" faraway lands in order to trade goods. This business really took off in the tiny Netherlands, which was a leading world power back then. The goal for ships from the Netherlands was to visit Asia and Africa in order to obtain highly valued spices, silks and other items. Mounting overseas voyages like this was very expensive and very risky in those days. There was a very real probability that a given vessel would be lost at sea. While some would try to raise money by appealing to the monarchs that ruled most European countries at the time, Holland was a vibrant and free economy. Some smart people had the idea of forming a company to mount overseas voyages, and selling pieces, or shares, of the company to the general public. They formed the Dutch East India Company and began selling *stock* in the company to the general public, which meant that people could buy shares to own a small portion of the company. As part of their ownership, they would be entitled to a proportionate share of any profits that the company earned.

As soon as you sell something, a secondary market develops for it. This was true of stocks as well. Rather than selling shares back to the company, people began selling their shares to others, often for a higher price than what they paid for them in the first place. This was the birth of the first stock markets. Pretty soon, stock markets became organized places where people could trade their shares. The modern concepts of stock markets and trading developed quickly, with people profiting from appreciation in the share prices themselves, not just from the profits that the company was paying. Soon enough, lots of companies were offering shares of stock, and the concept spread into other countries.

The Modern Stock Market and Dividends

The concepts developed back then have not changed much, but as the centuries went by the concept of offering stock in a company has matured, become regulated, and become centralized. By the 20th century, official stock markets had come into existence including the New York Stock exchange that played a central role in selling stock. Also, the idea of a publicly traded company, as opposed to a privately held company evolved. A publicly traded company sells shares of stock to the general public, and anyone with the money can buy those shares on one of the major stock exchanges. This is actually done through a brokerage, which is a company that provides members of the general public with a means to open accounts used for stock trading. You can deposit money in one of these accounts and use it to place orders to buy or sell shares of stock. The brokerage actually carries out the transactions for you in the stock exchanges. For this service, most charge a small fee per transaction called a commission. After the Great Depression, stock markets became highly regulated. In the United States this was done by the newly formed Securities and Exchange Commission. It is hard to say whether in total the regulations are protecting investors, but they do provide some assurance that companies that are publicly traded are being honest about their financial situation. As a result of regulation companies must file several audited reports on their assets, liabilities, income, and profits among other things. These reports can be used to determine the financial health of the company and whether it is worth investing in or not. While this works in most cases, many companies that were based on fraud, like WorldCom and Enron manage to fall through the cracks occasionally. But those are very rare events and transparency has been maintained on the stock markets.

So, let us get to the question of dividends. The first thing to ask is the most basic question of all, and that is what is a dividend? If you recall from our discussion of the Dutch East India Company, it paid out proportionate shares of it is profits to people who owned stock in the company. Those payments of profits are what we call dividends today.
So, if you ask what is a dividend, the short answer is it is a payment of the company's profits that you receive if you own shares of stock in the company. Dividends are typically paid out on a quarterly basis. You can look up important information about the dividends paid by a company that will

give you an idea of how worthwhile owning the stock is. Items to consider are:

- Dividend Payment: This is the amount in dollars per share. So, to get a particular annual income from a given stock, you can look up their annual dividend payment. Then figure out how many shares you need to own. For example, if a company pays a dividend of $4 per share, and you would like to make $6,000/year off the stock, you need to own $6,000/$4 = 1,500 shares of the stock. Note that dividends are paid quarterly, so to determine how much you would receive with each dividend payment, divide the quoted annual payment by four.

- Yield: This is the same concept as "interest rate" for a savings account or CD. Yield is calculated on a per share basis, however. On most stock market websites, yield is going to be calculated for you and displayed, but you can calculate it yourself by taking the dividend payment and dividing it by the stock price. As an example, consider Abbvie (ABBV), which currently has a dividend payment of $4.28 and a stock price of $65. The yield is $4.28/$65 x 100 = 6.6%. However, note that most sites are going to quote the *forward* yield. This is the expected yield in the coming year. That might be effected by either changes in the expected dividend payment, or changes in the stock price. Of course, those are estimates, but you are going to find that the current yield is pretty close to the forward yield.

- Ex-Dividend Date: Each quarter, the company will declare a date when dividends will be paid. They are also going to declare a record date. That is the date that shareholders are recorded to receive dividend payments. This is done to determine who owns the stock at the right time to receive the payments, and accounts for trading of shares. To be recorded, you must own the stock on the ex-Dividend date, which typically occurs two days before the date of record. As a long-term investor in dividend stocks, you should not be selling off shares very often, although there will be reasons to exit a position on occasion. To avoid unexpected problems with this, make sure that if you sell shares, you wait until the dividend payment has passed so that you receive that payment. If you are buying shares, make sure to try and buy them before the ex-dividend date.
- Payout ratio: This is dividend per share divided by earnings per share. This gives you an idea of the ability of a company to keep paying the current level of dividends. Any company with a payout ratio approaching or worse exceeding a 100% payout ratio is

14

going to be one that you want to avoid, unless there are specific reasons to believe that the situation will change in your favor going ahead. The pharmaceutical company Abbvie has a payout ratio of 47%. This is a good number, that indicates it is able to make the dividend payments and there is quite a bit of room to increase the dividend payments. A company with a payout ratio of 90% or over 100% is probably not going to be able to keep up the current dollar amount per share when it comes to paying their dividends.

- Dividend Growth: This is the number of consecutive years that the dividend payment has increased. The more years of dividend growth you see, the better the investment is. For example, the pharmaceutical company Abbvie has a dividend growth of 46 years. That is a very good track record that means the company is probably worth investing in to help secure your retirement income.

- Share price: Finally you need to know the share price. For a given dividend payment, this is going to give you an idea of how much it is going to cost in order to get the kind of income that you are looking for. It is important to avoid looking for so-called bargains, because a low share price betrays weakness in the stock in most cases. But you will have to weigh share price against other factors when making your selections.

If you understand the items described in this section, then you understand the fundamentals you need to know in order to determine if a given stock that pays dividends is a good investment. There are going to be many other factors to consider of course, and we will talk about that in chapter 8, where we will discuss fundamental analysis. This is a type of analysis that looks at the fundamentals of the company, such as profits, inventory, assets, and liabilities, to determine if the company is a good investment.

Yield is Important, but Betware

You want a dividend stock that pays a good yield, after all interest rate income is what you are really after with dividend stocks. However, yield is not the only factor to consider. You want yields that are average to slightly above average. If there are really high yields, this can be a red flag. Often, stocks that offer very high yields are not good stocks, and they are offering the high yields in order to entice investors into buying shares of their otherwise unappealing stocks. You are going to see many stocks with yields over 10%, even approaching 15% or 18%. You should view these kinds of stocks in the same way you'd view junk bonds. While you can always sell your shares to get out of a stock, keep in mind that it might be hard to get out of an undesirable stock – you still have to find a buyer. And the stock might crash at some point, if it hasn't already. Many stocks that offer very high yields are under $10 a share, and many are even penny stocks. A dividend investor should be careful, conservative, and methodical. That means that you are probably going to be avoiding penny stocks in your investments – or at least you should. Stick to large, mature, and largely blue chip companies. We will also talk about investing in exchange traded funds, which will widen your options because the company offering the fund will mitigate your risks by investing in tens to hundreds of companies at once.

History of Dividend Payments

One thing you are going to want to check is to look at the history of a company's dividend payments. Are they steady, declining, or increasing? A company with increasing dividend payments is preferred. Remember that we are always battling inflation in a modern economy, and if a dividend payment is not growing with time, it is losing value as a result of inflation. So, you certainly do not want a company with static or declining dividend payments unless there are some very good reasons from the fundamental analysis to believe that the situation is going to reverse in the future.

Something else to consider is how the company handled dividend payments during past economic downturns. If you find that the company used a downturn as an excuse to slash dividend payments, you might want to dig deeper. Did they raise payments back up to the previous level as soon as the recession was over? Or did they use the recession as an excuse to keep dividend payments at a new, lower level? Some companies will hold steady with their dividend payments during economic downturns. These are definitely solid companies to invest in.

Stock Price

It is tempting to seek out bargains. However, you pay for things one way or another, and if a stock has a low price per share, that is an indication that the stock is not necessarily the best one to invest in. When you are looking for dividend stocks to consider, you might invest in some value stocks. We will discuss what that really means in chapter 4. However, a low share price by itself does not convey "value". Beware of stocks that are cheap, below $30 a share. There are some good stocks that might be lower priced, but they have to be evaluated thoroughly. Mature companies that are good investments are typically going to have share prices of $50 or more, and in most cases over $100 per share.

Not All Stocks Pay Dividends – Here's Why

One of the curious things about the stock market for new dividend investors is why some stocks do not pay dividends at all. In many cases, these are highly recognized and prized stocks like Amazon, Netflix, or Google. What is going on here? Remember what a dividend is. The company is paying out a share of it is profits to investors, often most of it is profits. In order to be in a position to do that, the company must be mature, have large value, and have a solid grip on the market it is involved in. That does not mean it has to be a monopoly, that is not the case at all. But it has to have a solid market share that is relatively stable. More to the point, it must have enough market share that it is not aggressively seeking growth. That can include market share here at home as well as market share overseas, in other mature markets like Europe and Japan and in developing markets as well.

Many older companies are still growing, but their plan for growth is slow and steady. They are probably investing a lot in research and development, and they are interested in holding their market position while growing it in a sustainable fashion. These types of companies are able to pay dividends. This includes companies like Boeing, Chevron, Abbvie, Apple, IBM, Amgen, and Microsoft.

In contrast, some companies are in an aggressive growth phase. The younger the company the more likely it is seeking very aggressive growth. These days, this includes most (but not all) of the high-tech companies. Facebook, Google, Twitter, Tesla, and Amazon are some examples that come to mind. In order to grow fast and penetrate markets, these companies plow all of their profits back into the company. They may even be experiencing losses right now, like Tesla is and Amazon did for many years. Since these companies are spending every cent that comes in, they do not pay dividends. Of course, this does not mean the stock is not worth owning. Stock in these companies has appreciated in value by a huge amount and is likely to keep doing so for many more years if not decades. That means they can be a good investment for other reasons. And, if you load up on shares now, that could pay off down the road, either selling them for a profit or potentially as the companies mature, they may start paying dividends.

However, that kind of investment is not the topic of this book. Our focus in this book is finding companies that pay dividends and investing in those. If earning a dividend income is your goal, you should be laser focused and avoid investing in stocks based in hypotheticals. While the odds are good that many of the companies noted such as Amazon or Netflix will probably appreciate in value over the years, and at some point, they might pay dividends, these are both hypothetical and therefore high-risk propositions. In contrast, investing in a mature company that has a history of paying good dividends and that is in a good evergreen market, is one that is much lower risk.

How to Find Dividend Paying Stocks

Finding dividend paying stocks is actually easy. You can visit any stock market website and look up stock tickers. For each stock, the site is going to list certain properties of the share like the P/E ratio (price to earnings ratio). They will also list other important properties of the stock – including whether or not they pay dividends. This is easy to spot because it will say N/A (not applicable) if a company does not pay dividends when it comes to yield and payment, along with ex-dividend date. If yield, payment, and ex-dividend date are listed, this indicates that the stock pays dividends.

You can also visit dividend.com, the world's leading website when it comes to finding stocks that pay dividends, and evaluating the key statistics associated with dividend stocks like yield, share price, payout ratio, and annual dividend payment. You have to pay for a membership to get access to all the features, but they offer most of the important features free of charge. You can also pull up lists of dividend stocks, such as those paying the highest yields, or those paying the highest annual payouts.

We will talk more about investment strategies later, but building a solid portfolio consisting of a diverse but limited set of investments is the way to go. So, you can use these sites together with fundamental analysis (chapter 8) in order to pick out the stocks you want to invest in as a part of your plan.

Chapter 2: Why You Should Invest in Dividend Stocks

There are many different strategies that can be used in the stock market. Some people simply hope to profit from the price appreciation of the shares. Over the long term, share prices of stock almost always appreciate. This means that you can build up a large portfolio of shares, and then when you are ready to retire you can start selling your shares in small bits at a time and take cash profits. Then you can live off the cash. Investors that use this strategy are probably not going to be interested in dividend stocks.

Others try and get short term profits. People who buy and sell stocks for short term profits are known as traders. A trader is someone that buys stock at a perceived low price, and then they wait for the price to rise to an acceptable level of profits, and they sell their shares. Of course, we are describing the ideal situation, trading stocks for profits is a lot harder than it sounds. Most day traders lose, rather than earn money.

Dividend investors want to hold onto their stocks. A dividend investor is investing in order to receive the cash payments that the stock offers through dividends. So, these are income generating investments. As a dividend investor, the only real time that you would consider selling off shares of stock is when the company begins underperforming or worse. If a company maintains it is market share and performance, you might keep your ownership of the stock indefinitely. Your goal is to be able to generate significant income from dividend payments, possibly using them for all of your living expenses.

In this chapter, we are going to spend some time talking about the why of dividend investing in more detail. We are going to use the concept of compound interest to show how growing investments can explode in value when you reinvest your earnings. The general strategy used by dividend investors is to reinvest the dividend payments when you are still working and able to receive income from other sources, so that you can grow your investment at maximal capacity. This will involve growing it by purchasing new shares of stock on a regular basis, and also reinvesting your dividend payments to buy even more shares of stock. This way, with each passing quarter, your investments are significantly growing, setting the stage for a good, solid income when you decide to stop growing your investments, and retire. At that point you can live off the dividend income and any other sources of income you have like social security.

Retirement income, and am I too old?

Imagine the financial freedom, however. So many people today are relying on a small 401k plan, that they may hardly pay attention to or even understand. They also hope to get money from social security payments. Compare this to the possibility of building up a solid portfolio of dividend stocks that is going to pay you large amounts of money ten, twenty, or thirty years from now when you retire.

No matter your age, you should consider investing in dividend stocks. Of course, the older you are, the more aggressive you are going to have to be in order to make it work. It is always possible to get some income from dividend stocks no matter how old you are. If you are in your fifties or even early sixties, if you are in good physical condition and expect to be able to continue working, you can invest aggressively and build up a nice portfolio that you can use to assist with your living expenses in retirement. If you are 50 or over, you are probably not going to be able to completely rely on a dividend stock portfolio. Therefore, older investors who are behind and need to start building up their investments will have to be very aggressive. This will mean investing a significant fraction of the money that you can invest in stocks that do not pay dividends but that have a high probability of appreciating in value. Later, you can either cash out these stocks and take the cash to live on, or you can reinvest the money at that time, after the principal has grown, into dividend paying stocks, and then you can collect income at that time. But the point is you will probably not get to a point of making a significant income only investing in slow growth stocks, because it does take a significant amount of capital.

Many financial strategists recommend allocating an investment portfolio by percentages. This book is not offering investment advice, so you will have to consult your own investment advisor or use your own judgment when building your portfolio. But a possibility to consider is that you should invest about 65-70% of your income in high growth stocks that do not pay dividends if you are 50 or older, and 30-35% in dividend paying stocks. If you are disciplined and able to keep up your investment program, as you approach a point where you are considering retiring you can start moving your portfolio more to dividend paying stocks.

For stocks that you are looking to grow wealth simply from appreciation in share price, the general rule, if you are going to hold those stocks, is to sell about 4% of your portfolio every year to take out the cash. However, this is only a suggestion and we cannot give anyone advice because we do not know the specific situations of any readers, and situations are going to differ from investor to investor. But one idea is to start selling off your stocks after they have appreciated in value, and then begin buying up more shares of dividend paying stocks to ensure that you get the quarterly income from the stocks. That way you can start generating income while staying fully invested.

Those who are younger have a good time horizon to build up a dividend portfolio over time. If you are 45 or younger, you can afford to be more conservative and focus on a program of slowly building up a large dividend portfolio.

Compound Interest

The concept of compound interest is often taught in algebra classes, but unfortunately most people forget about it by the time they reach adulthood. Compound interest illustrates the power of saving and investing. When money can earn interest, and the interest is reinvested, that "compounds" the investment each time interest is earned. Over time, this means that if you also continue to make regular contributions to the investment, it will grow exponentially. This simple concept used to mean you could put money in the bank and thirty years later have a million dollars. These days, since banks do not pay hardly anything, they aren't worth using except to stash some cash away for emergency situations. But fortunately for us dividend stocks can play this role.

Dividend stocks actually do it better. When you put money into a bank or CD, the principal that you invest – the original amount of money that you put into the account – actually loses value. This is because of inflation, the ever-present and relatively silent tax that causes the value of money to decline each and every year. In recent decades inflation has been low, but it is still not zero and it eats away at your principal. In order to make profits, you need to have an interest rate that accounts for the inflation rate first, and then adds on top of that. To account for inflation, it is got to be at least 2-3%.

Looking up some CD interest rates for Ally bank, they are paying between 2.3% - 2.6% interest (note that these values are constantly changing, and so they only hold for the time of writing). If inflation is around 2%, that means you are barely earning any money at all investing in these types of financial instruments. At best, it is a way to preserve some money for safety.

In contrast, a stock like IBM has a yield over 4%.

But dividend stocks go beyond paying "interest". The principal invested in a stock typically grows with time. So for example, in 1995 IBM was around $25 a share. Today it is trading for $140 per share. Not all stocks are always going to appreciate like that, but if you have been investing in IBM, the value of your original investment has grown considerably due to the appreciation of the share price of the stock, and you are also receiving the dividend payments which play the same role as interest does in a savings account or bank CD. So dividend stocks could be said to have compounding compound interest, rather than just compound interest.

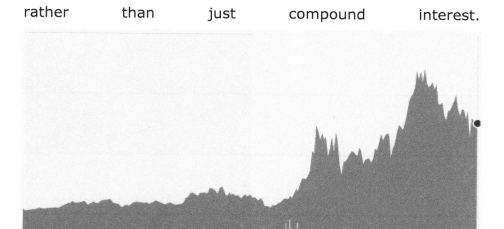

This chart shows the growth of IBM share price over time.

Now let us consider how compound interest can grow your money. In the following example, we assume that you start off with $1,000, and that you invest an additional $500 per month. Over the course of ten years, with an interest rate of 4%, at the end of the period you would have $75,000.

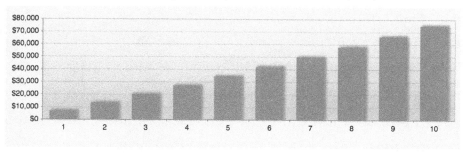

If you started with $10,000, invested $500 a month with 4% interest, at the end of 20 years, you would have $204,428.

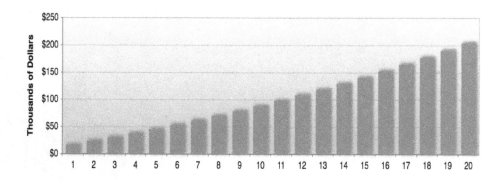

In order to see how dividend stocks would grow in value, we need to consider the stock appreciation in addition to the interest payment. This can result in an effective interest of 7%, or even 10% of more. The S & P 500 appreciates in value around 7% a year, but we do not have to use an aggressive number like that. Let's suppose that the combined dividend yield and annual appreciation of the shares added up to 8%. Now we'll reconsider that same 20-year investment, with an additional investment of $500 a month. That change alone would add more than $100,000 to your account at the end of the 20-year period.

This is important because in order to maintain the yield, dividend paying stocks are going to increase the amount they pay in proportion to the stock appreciation, and many will go beyond that. This means that the value of your portfolio in terms of the worth of the shares is going to be as important as the dividend yield (interest rate).

Upping the amount, you invest each month matters to. If your total interest rate including appreciation plus dividend yield was 8%, but you invested $1,000 each month instead of $500 to buy new shares, at the end of 20 years your account would be worth more than $600,000.

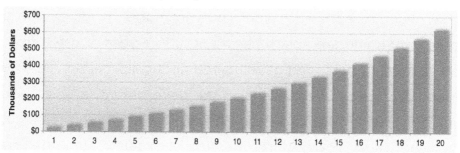

Even at the end of ten years, you would have an account worth more than $200,000. That indicates that older investors can benefit from an aggressive approach as well.

Passive Income and Financial Freedom

Of course, the earlier you start the better, but the benefit of dividend stocks is quite apparent. They are going to provide you with passive income. Each quarter, after you have accumulated enough shares so that you are satisfied with the size of your portfolio, you will receive regular and reliable dividend payments in the form of cash. This can form a part of your strategy for passive income. For those who are able to accumulate enough shares to earn a middle-class level income or higher, they may be able to get all of their income from dividend stocks alone. Anything above that like social security payments will be an added benefit, rather than something you have to depend on to scrimp by.

Many investors will have to use a combination of aggressive growth stocks and dividend stocks to get the amount of money they want to earn each year. But no matter what path you take, when you are able to earn $50,000 a year or more from stock investments, you have gained financial freedom. At that point you are not dependent on the government, a boss, or a job for your income. You can choose to work if you want to, but you will not be required to work in order to survive. This is what financial freedom is all about, being able to live happily and comfortably without depending on others for your income.

How much do I have to invest?

It is going to be important to have some general idea of how many shares you need to buy in order to attain different levels of income from dividend payments. Of course, the situation is dynamic, that is, it is always changing and so we cannot rely on a quick estimate today in order to determine what we really need ten or twenty years from now. However, the estimates are going to be fairly accurate.

Let US start at $20,000. While later we are going to advise that investors build a highly diversified portfolio, for the sake of example we will consider a single stock for the exercises in this section. Let us consider the pharmaceutical company Abbvie. IT IS a very popular one with investors, and there are good reasons for this. First off, Abbvie is a company that is more than 100 years old. Second, it has a 46-year record of increasing dividend payments. The yield is 6.53%, much higher than the interest rates that you will find at banks these days. The annual pay out per share is $4.28. The payout ratio is 54.5%, indicating the company is healthy as far as paying dividends goes, and it has a lot of room to grow.

It is currently trading at $65 a share. Of course, ten years from now the number is possibly going to be very different, but how much would you need to invest if you wanted a $20,000 income right now?

With a $4.28 payout per share, this would require:

$20,000/$4.28 = 4,673 shares

This would cost:

4,673 x $65 = $303,745

Hopefully this number does not shock readers. It is a realistic number, and the amount you have to invest is dependent on yield and it is going to be relatively constant no matter what stocks you pick, unless you go for outliers.

From this calculation, we can see that, to earn $50,000 a year from this stock, we have to invest $759,000. What this exercise shows is that unless you have a large amount of capital available already, you are going to have to build up a dividend portfolio for income purposes over a period of time. If you do not own any dividend paying stocks, there is not a better time than right now to get started.

To earn $100,000 a year from Abbvie, you would have to buy 23,365 shares. That would cost $1.5 million.

Some stocks pay much higher annual payouts. Creditor LTD (BAC) for example, pays $20 dividends per share. The price of the stock is $205. To make $20,000 a year from this stock, you would have to buy 1,000 shares. This would cost $205,000. That is nearly a third less than the cost of Abbvie, but the payout ratio is an unhealthy 126%. That means it would take some investigation to determine whether or not that is a good stock to invest in. It may be that the company will be able to keep up the dividend payments because it is slated for future growth, but you are also risking the fact those high $20 payouts per share are going to be dropping significantly in the future. Abbvie is a safer investment.

Reinvesting Your Dividend Income and DRIPS

The discussion in this section will not apply if you already have a large amount of capital to invest. In that case, you can buy the number of shares that you need for your desired income level and start enjoying your dividend income.

However, if you are just getting started with your investing, your dividend investing plan will involve two distinct phases.

The first phase is going to be the one that you use to build up the number of shares that you own. Depending on how aggressive you are in your stock purchases and how much you can put in every month, this period of time can last anywhere from years to several decades. During this phase, you are not going to be interested in taking out money for income and we are assuming that you have some other source of income you are able to live on for now and use to invest. That means that you should be trying to accumulate as many shares as possible. One way to go about doing this is to take all the money you receive as dividend income and reinvest it in more share purchases. This procedure should continue until you enter the second and final phase of your dividend investment plan, which is when you can relax and collect the dividend payments each quarter to use as income.

So, a dividend investment plan generally has two phases – the investment phase and the income phase.

During the investment phase, you can either rely on your own discipline to reinvest money, or you can set things up so that it is done on your behalf. If you can do so, you should enroll in a DRIP, which is a Dividend ReInvestment Plan. When you enroll in DRIPs, your dividends are automatically used to buy more shares. So, if you have shares of Chevron, when the dividends are paid, rather than giving you the cash the money will be used to buy more shares of Chevron instead. These types of plans not only enforce discipline by making sure that you are actually using the money in order to buy more shares, they also allow you to buy fractional shares. That may not sound appealing, but over the years purchases of fractional shares are going to add up to real dividend money. Especially if you are investing over a period of ten years or more.

So, if you were investing in IBM at $140 a share, and you made $70 in dividend income in a given quarter, rather than pocketing the $70 a DRIP would allow you to purchase ½ of a share. Over one year, that would be an additional four shares of IBM stock, in addition to any that you bought on your own as part of your continued investment plan.

And the more shares that you own over time, the larger your share purchases made using DRIPs is doing to become.

The Importance of Having a Plan

One of the problems that plagues new self-directed investors is that they start buying stocks without any real investment plan. That is one of the worst things you can do. You need to set goals and then devise a plan to reach them. Keep in mind that the plan does not have to be written on stone tablets. As circumstances change, you can adjust the plan as necessary. Hopefully as time goes on you have more money to invest, and you can increase your regular stock purchases, allowing you to build up a larger portfolio.

The first aspect of an investment plan is doing your dividend analysis (chapter 1), your fundamental analysis (chapter 8), and maintaining a strategy for successful investing (chapter 4). From here you will pick stocks to invest in.

The second aspect of your plan is to decide for yourself how many shares of stock you are going to buy at regular intervals. Having the discipline to create this type of plan and sticking to it is often what makes the difference between success or failure.

In the beginning, you do not have to set large goals. When first starting out you want to develop habits first. So, if you are only buying one share of stock a week, it does not matter, it is more important to start buying one share of stock a week and then turning that into a habit. Later on, down the road, you can start buying two shares a week, then three shares, and so on. Do not think in terms of having to do it all at once. Of course you do not want to be super conservative to the point of it being a detriment, at some point if you are going to accumulate enough shares of stock in order to build up enough dividend income to live on, you are going to need to be more aggressive. But you have to start somewhere, and so IT IS good to start with a stock in a mid-price range (Maybe $50-

$80 a share) and buy one share at regular intervals until you are ready to do more.

People who are desperate to get going can blow a lot of money at once and make mistakes. Even if you are a late starter in your investment career, it is recommended that you start off slowly and methodically and build up a solid process. You do not need to put every penny you have in right away; you want to have a solid pattern of behavior that is sustainable over the long term.

Tax Implications of a Dividend Lifestyle

Dividends are generally not taxed at the capital gains rate. First of all, you will have to determine if dividend payments that you are receiving are qualified or unqualified dividends.

For qualified dividends, the income is taxed as capital gains. The capital gains tax rate is either 15% or 20% for most people, depending on your total income. Most dividends that you receive from U.S. corporations are taxed as qualified dividends, and so you will be able to pay the capital gains tax rate, which is not only lower but simpler to manage.

There are certain holding requirements. You must hold the stock for at least 60 days prior to the ex-dividend date in order to qualify for the capital gains tax treatment. Dividends that are paid from REITS (real estate investment trusts), MLPs (master limited partnerships) or BDCs (Business Development

Companies) are unqualified dividends, but some of those investments have other tax advantages.

If you have held a stock for less than 60 days prior to the ex-dividend date, then the payment will be treated as unqualified for taxation purposes, at least for that quarter. This means that you will have to pay regular income taxes on any dividend income you receive under those conditions.

For most dividend investors, these tax issues are not going to be important. This is because you will have held your investment for many years before you start taking income from it, so all of your dividends are going to be qualified dividends in that case.

Chapter 3: Finding a Brokerage and Implementing Your Investment Plans

After you have done some research and arrived at a few stocks that you want to invest in for the purposes of getting dividend income, it is time to start implementing your plans. The first step in doing so is going to be finding the right broker. To a certain extent, finding the right broker is a matter of personal taste. These days most brokers offer fairly similar services, and so it might even boil down to what user interface you like best. One issue to consider is whether you prefer trading on a desktop computer or using a mobile device such as a phone or tablet.

Another issue which can be described as classic is the commission charged by the broker. A commission is a fee the broker charges in order to execute trades on your behalf. For dividend investors, who are not going

to be trading very frequently, this is less of an issue than it is for other types of investors. For example, day traders will be entering and exiting many trades during the day and so will be very concerned with issues like commissions, which can really eat into their profits if they are doing a lot of trades.

Once you get setup with a broker, you want to start implementing your investment plans. This is going to be something that you have to stick to on a regular basis. Everyone is going to have their own schedule, and that will be determined in part by the way you earn your income and when money to invest becomes available. But the most important aspect of this is to make sure you are investing regularly.

Choosing the Right Brokerage

At this point in time, the brokerage market has somewhat matured. So, it probably is not going to be an issue for you to find brokers that have a mobile app, for example. Second, since dividend investing is not an hour by hour or minute by minute activity the way trading is, having access to a full suite of tools that lets you do chart analysis probably is not going to be something you are worried about.

The biggest factors are probably going to be cost and ease of use. Most brokerages charge a commission to execute trades, but these days there are a few that offer zero commission trades. This is a nice feature, who would not argue with free? One example of a zero-commission brokerage is Robinhood. It is a relatively new brokerage, and it has a very easy to use mobile app interface. You can also access it is investing tools online. Robinhood lacks the type of analysis tools that you would get with some of the trading sites that are in part geared toward day traders and such, but as we have mentioned before those kinds of tools are irrelevant to dividend investors.

For some dividend investors, stability of the company might be an issue. There are several older brokerages that are still around and doing very well. Among these are Charles Schwab and Fidelity Investments. These are well-known and stable companies, so you might be willing to pay the small commission fees to run your investments through these brokers. They may also have help including financial advice available depending on what type of plan you sign up for, which may or may not be helpful.

Other well-known brokers that have not been around quite as long but are still mature include TD Ameritrade and E*Trade. TD Ameritrade was founded in the early 1970s, and E*Trade was founded about a decade earlier.

Ally Invest, run by Ally Bank is also another well-known option that appeals to many investors.

For those that charge commissions, they are more than likely going to charge fees that are in roughly the same ballpark. You are probably looking at $5-7 per trade. That does not sound like much, but it can add up. If you are looking to be a long-term investor, it probably is not going to amount to much when all is said and done, but you will need to account for it when you are determining whether or not your investments are profitable or not.

There are other zero commission brokers besides Robinhood. M1 Finance is an interesting alternative. Not only is it zero commission, M1 Finance allows you to invest in fractional shares. This can be an option for those who are cash strapped at the present time, you can use that ability to at least get something in your portfolio.

Account Minimums

Some brokers have account minimums. For example, E*Trade requires a minimum balance of $500. Some are pay as you go. Once you've connected your bank account, you can transfer money on the fly with Robinhood. The account minimum is one thing that you are going to want to look into before you tie yourself up with a broker. Some may have higher account minimums, and for most people a $500 requirement is not going to be a huge obstacle to worry about. But as part of the overall picture you do need to consider every penny that you have to spend. If you are just starting out and you only have $200 but you're anxious to start getting some stocks under your belt, then going with a brokerage that requires a $500 minimum might not be worth waiting around for. In that case you might just go ahead and get started with Robinhood, so that you can at least start buying some shares and getting your investment portfolio going.

The Bottom Line When Choosing a Brokerage

There are not really differences that are all that significant between brokerages when it comes to dividend investing. As we have said, as a dividend investor you are not going to be all that concerned with fancy tools like stock charts with technical indicators. One thing that people ask about is the issue of financial reports. The financials that you are going to be interested in when it comes to doing fundamental analysis of a company you might be investing in are available for free online. So, a broker having them there is not really offering anything that you cannot get anywhere else. For one thing, they should be readily available on the company website. For example, various reports and filings that are require by the SEC for Apple are available for public access here:

https://investor.apple.com/investor-relations/default.aspx

You can also get forms of this nature, at least brief summaries, from stock market sites that are free to access like Yahoo

Finance. You can also get a lot of important information from dividend.com. So, this should not be an issue.

Since every penny count, although commissions are not all that expensive, you might consider going with a zero-commission broker. That way you can engage in a lot of trades without having to worry about mounting fees, even if they average out over the long term.

What Happens if a Broker Goes Under?

Something people new to individual investing might be wondering what happens if a broker goes out of business or if it closes down for other reasons. Often, arrangements might be made to simply transfer your account to a different broker. Once thing you might want to verify is whether or not your brokerage belongs to the Securities Investor Protection Corp (SPIC). This organization insures investments in stocks and bonds, up to $500,000. Up to $250,000 of this can be cash.

But remember that when you buy shares of stock, you own shares in the company, and the broker is just a middleman. If the broker ends up going out of business, that should not have any impact on shares of stock that you own in different companies.

The concern with a broker going completely under would be any cash that you had in your account with them. That is where the real risk lies. If you plan on moving large amounts of cash at a single time into your brokerage account, then you might check to see if the broker you selected is SPIC insured.

Just keep in mind that the stock you own stays with you, and the value of the stock is determined by the value of the company and the brokerage has nothing to do with that part.

How to Buy Stocks

Buying and selling stocks is as easy as renting a movie. You simply look up the stock you want and then determine how many shares you want to purchase and place your order. One thing to note is that there are two types of orders. These are called market orders and limit orders.

Most people execute market orders. If you look up a stock and just click the buy button, then that is a market order. It is going to buy the stock for you at the prevailing market price as soon as it is able to do so. Market orders usually execute quickly.

If you are interested in trying to save money, you can place a limit order. This type of order will only fill if the limit price that you specify is taken by a buyer or seller. Using a limit order, investors can try to buy stocks at discount prices, provided they can find someone willing to sell at the limit order price. A limit order also allows you to wait until market conditions actually change so that the stock price drops to your limit price.

Limit orders can be entered as good until the end of the trading day, or good until canceled.

Limit orders are very useful for traders who are not looking to hold stock for very long for various reasons. However, for a dividend investor wasting energy on limit orders is probably not the best way to spend your efforts. Most dividend investors are simply going to be placing market orders.

In the following chapter, we are going to talk about important investment strategies. Part of this will be buying your stocks at regular intervals. It is not the job of the dividend investor to try and guess which way the stock is moving, leave that insanity to the traders. Over the course of years that you invest, temporary ups and downs are going to average out and not be all that important for your overall investing.

While the more frequently you buy stocks the better, sticking to some kind of schedule is more important. Some people might only buy stocks once a month, and that is fine. Others might buy every two weeks whenever they get paid. Still others might buy once a week. Again, the time frame you use is not as important as setting up a plan and sticking to it. If you get in the habit of regular investing, this is going to make it more likely that by the time you reach your retirement you are going to have a solid portfolio that can produce the kind of income you want.

Setting Your Income Goals

In the last chapter we touched a little bit on how many shares you would need in order to reach a given income goal. You should keep that in mind when you start buying shares. If you buy one share a month, and you need 4,500 shares to meet your goal, that probably is not going to work out for you since it would take 375 years. So you need to look at how many shares you are going to need in order to reach the desired level of income, and then break that down into a set of share purchases that can be put on a regular schedule that will also be something that can be realized within the time limits that you have set for yourself. So, if you only have ten years to invest and you need 4,500 shares, that means that you are going to have to buy 450 shares a year. That translates into about 38 shares a month. Depending on the stock, this can be an expensive proposition. So, it is better to start out early in your investment life so that you can actually realize your goals. As we said in the first two chapters, if you are in a situation where you are getting older but still want dividend income, chances are you are going to have to use a high growth portfolio now instead. Then when you reach retirement age you can start selling shares from your high growth stocks and buy dividend paying shares at that time. At least you will have more capital to work with. A compromise setup would be to invest 65% in high growth stocks and 35% in dividend stocks, so that you are acquiring shares of high growth stocks while also starting to build up a dividend portfolio at the same time.

It is important to be realistic about meeting your goals. Also do not be too concerned about short term fluctuations, and even recessions. Most downturns are short-lived. You should not try and estimate the annual return for a stock when it is in the midst of a downturn, and then think it is a bad deal. You will need to look at the overall growth of the company.

For those looking to get a good middle-class income from their dividend stocks, a good goal to set is acquiring 10,000 shares of stock. For most people that do not have thousands of dollars to throw into the stock market every month, this is not going to be an easy feat to accomplish. Just like the previous example – it is going to take a long time, and you are going to have to buy the lots in small increments. This is why it is always far better to start investing early in life. Unfortunately, our high schools and universities do not teach students about financial management and investing, and most people are financially illiterate. Many of us did not grow up knowing much about finances and how to secure our future because our parents did not know either. That makes it hard for many people to plan. As you have probably heard on the news from time to time, most Americans do not even have the ability to come up with $400 to pay for a minor emergency. So, most people are not even remotely thinking about a long-term investment plan that can secure their long-term future. If that describes the situation that you have come from, do not feel bad. You are taking the first steps by reading books like this so that you can turn your financial life around and secure a better future, even if the road to that better future is going to be more difficult that it would have been had you started early. If you are over the age of 50 and you find it difficult to put in significant amounts of money to invest, you might even consider getting a second job. It is better to work more now when you are physically able to do so, than it is to try and stretch out your working life when you might not have the capacity. Then you can take all the income from the second job and use that to start an aggressive investment program. If you are able to put in $1,000 a month, over ten years that would amount to $120,000 invested. If you could put $2,000 a month, that would amount to $240,000 invested. You could buy 3,692 shares in Abbvie with that money and have a supplemental income of about $15,000 a year – which would be a great addition to social security income.

There are many possibilities and situations, and everyone is going to have a unique story. But no matter what situation you find yourself in it should be possible to find a way to a better future, provided that you begin taking action. The point here is not to discourage people from investing in dividend stocks because the amount needed can be hard to realize, but rather to get people to see the situation realistically.

Chapter 4: Investment Strategies

In this chapter we are going to take a look at the main investment strategies used by long-term investors. The buy-and-hold investment community includes dividend investors. There are several strategies that are used, the main approach is to avoid investing too much into a single stock or small number of stocks, in order to avoid going down if that one investment ends up turning bad. Secondly, you want to avoid buying at the wrong time. Although traders may try and wow you with all their signals and magic tricks, it is virtually impossible to know whether or not he market has reached the top or bottom, or when the trend is going to reverse. Over the long term even buying at price peaks can be lucrative, but we are going to show you a strategy that will help you avoid that folly. We are also going to talk about rebalancing your portfolio, if that is necessary in your case, and finally when to get out of a stock.

Types of Risk Faced by Investors

There are different types of risk that you are going to face as an investor. For example, you might invest in a company that becomes embroiled in scandal, and then it is share price might drop to penny stock levels. Or, you might be heavily invested when a large recession hits, and you will find that almost every stock is dropping in value by large amounts as investors race to the exits in a panic.

There are many other risks as well. There are risks related to the overall performance of the economy, risks related to inflation rates, and risks related to interest rates.

Some risks are directly related to the stock market, while others are not. Some have a major influence on the stock market, even though they are outside the stock market.

When a risk factor is outside the stock market, like GDP growth or the inflation rate, but it impacts every single stock, we say that this is systemic risk. These types of risk are not localized to a particular industry or stock, and these risks are largely out of the control of individuals.

Un-systemic risks are those that are specific to a particular company, industry, or sector. So, this can involve a problem impacting the banking sector, or maybe a problem impacting the tech sector. Sometimes there will be risks that only impact one or a few stocks, without impacting others. For example, you might see Netflix go down, while Facebook and Google go up. Maybe Netflix goes down because it lost a large number of subscribers. That could have a major impact on the share price of Netflix, but it will not have any impact on other companies. If anything, if it did have impact on other companies, you would imagine it might even help them out, if they offer any kind of competing service. For example, Apple and Amazon have Apple TV and Amazon Prime, respectively. These services might benefit if people are fleeing Netflix, and so the share prices of these companies might be rising when the share price of Netflix is in steep decline.

The main way that you can defend yourself against systemic risk is by using dollar cost averaging. That is not really the main purpose of dollar cost averaging, but it is something that is going to help your investments out when you are seeing downturns in the market. As we will see, dollar cost averaging should be used with a constant spend at regular intervals, so the kind of systemic risk that we are talking about is something that can be dealt with by purchasing shares during downturns.

Un-systemic risk is dealt with using diversification. If you spread out your investments, then you are not going to be nearly as sensitive to the ups and downs of one or two companies.

One way that many investors protect themselves against systemic risk is by diversifying by putting money in different classes of investments. So, they will hold some money in cash, put some money in government bonds, and put some money in corporate bonds. It is possible to do that while still pursuing a dividend investment strategy, but that really is not the focus of this book. So, if you are interested in putting some of your money in cash or bonds, please find an appropriate reference to help guide you on that journey.

Dollar Cost Averaging

Let us start by looking at one way that we can protect ourselves against systemic risk, although that really is not the purpose of this strategy. Dollar cost averaging helps us in multiple ways.

The first strategy that is used by long-term investors, and that should find it is way into the stock buying habits of anyone looking to buy a dividend stock, is dollar cost averaging. The goal of this strategy is to average out the ups and downs that naturally occur in the stock market over time. This also includes recessions and booms, which while intense at the time will look small compared to overall trends when you look back many years later.

Simply put, the stock market is full of volatility. What that means is prices are rapidly fluctuating up and down, in random fashion. The main purpose of dollar cost averaging is to reduce the impact of volatility on your purchasing. Dollar cost averaging will smooth out the prices you pay, so that you are basically buying your stocks at an average price.

The key to this strategy is to ensure that you are getting the best possible price for your purchases. Obviously, you do not want to be the investor that always buys at market peaks. Doing that would mean that you are spending the maximum amount possible for your stocks.

Studies have actually shown that if you invest over a long-time frame, even buying your stocks at market peaks is not something you have to be too concerned about. The long-term price trends are simply going to swamp the prices of stocks in the little hills and valleys they travel through as the stock market undergoes short term fluctuations.

If you have every looked at technical indicators, you will notice that you can plot moving averages on a stock chart. Although as a dividend investor you are not going to have to worry about such tools, it can be a good idea to put some moving averages on your stock chart to see how they look. You can think of dollar cost averaging as an attempt to buy stocks at the moving average price, when all is said and done. If you are buying stocks at regular intervals, you are going to find that sometimes you are buying shares at low prices, and sometimes you are buying shares at higher prices. But since you are buying shares all the time, these ups and downs in the prices that you pay are going to average out, and so if you look at your purchasing patterns in total, over the course of say a year, you are going to be paying the average price for the shares.

The more frequently that you make stock purchases, the closer that you are going to get to the average that you want to approach. If you purchase shares on the 15th of every month, that is good. But if you purchase shares on the 15th and the 30th of every month, that is even better. If you purchase shares every Friday, you are improving your odds even more. If you buy shares every day, that is the best scenario. You should have regular intervals in between your stock purchases, and you should not try buying your stocks looking for a bargain. The bargain price may never arrive in any timely fashion.

Dollar cost averaging does not just impact the price paid for shares. Under multiple scenarios, you can actually end up buying more shares over time using dollar cost averaging, as compared to making lump sum purchases. Rather than thinking in terms of the number of shares to purchase, when doing dollar cost averaging, think in terms of the amount of money that you are going to spend each time you buy stocks. Sometimes you are going to be buying more shares, and sometimes fewer shares.

- Set a specific amount that you can use to buy shares of stock.
- You should buy stocks at least once a month. If you do, pick a specific date that you use to buy stocks. You have to make a rule that you will not wait to buy hoping to obtain a better price. You have to go about this without injecting emotion, hopes, or wishes. Stick to the rule no matter what.
- If you are able to buy stocks more often, you should do so. Twice a month is better than once a month, and once a week is better than twice a month.

- Do not waver from your plan. Over time, it is all going to average out.

Let us look at a real-world example that shows you are better off using dollar cost averaging, in that you are actually going to end up with more shares. We will look at purchasing shares in Facebook over the course of a single year, using the actual stock prices. First let's suppose that you have $50,000 cash, and you decide to make a lump sum purchase at the beginning of the year. For $50,000, you will be able to buy 287 shares when the price is about $174 per share.

Now let us look at a dollar cost averaging plan. Rather than spending the entire $50,000 at once, you decide to spend $4,200 a month buying Facebook shares. We do not know how the stock is going to move over the course of an entire year, but we know the price is going to fluctuate up and down a lot over that time period. Using the actual data, it fluctuated between $124.95 a share and $204.87 a share. Purchasing on about the same day of the month, over the course of 12 months investing $4,200 a month we would have been able to buy the following numbers: 24 shares, 26 shares, 27 shares, 30 shares, 34 shares, 28 shares, 26 shares, 26 shares, 24 shares, 23 shares, 22 shares, 21 shares, and finally 23 shares. In total, we would own 334 shares by the end of the year. So, we would own 47 additional shares, which his 16% more shares than we would own had we bought the stock with a lump sum purchase. Imagine if you carry out that kind of stock purchasing plan over the course of five, ten, or twenty years. You would end up owning quite a few more shares, and you would also have averaged out the prices paid to buy the shares and so possibly have been better off. This example actually shows we were better off, because our friend who made the lump sum purchase was not able to take advantage of the routine price drops that occur with any stock.

Facebook does not pay a dividend, but what if it paid a $6 dividend like IBM? Those extra 47 shares a year would mean an extra $282, and over the course of 10 years we would be talking several thousand dollars, possibly up to $3,000 in extra dividend income.

So, dollar cost averaging is not some theory you should dismiss. It actually works and will lead to far better investment results, not only in the amount of dividend payments that you are going to be receiving several years down the line, but also in the number of shares you own in the present day.

Of course, in different years, there are going to be different scenarios. You are going to find yourself buying stock in a situation where the market is moving up. You are also going to find yourself buying stock when the market is moving down. Finally, there are going to be long time periods when the market is sideways. In each case, someone can make an argument against dollar cost averaging, but they will be wrong. The thing about price movements is nobody knows when they are going to occur or which direction they are going to go. As a long-term investor, you are not sweating the details.

Dollar cost averaging will help you avoid mistiming the market. This is a mistake that people constantly make, when they try and guess what the best time is to buy shares. People are usually wrong in their estimations. During a recent downturn, I had several people told me I was making a mistake buying shares. They said, "you need to wait, it is going to drop even more, and hasn't hit bottom." Guess what –they were wrong in their guessing game. Soon after the market went up again. I did not know whether or not the market was going up or down, but I do not care about things like that – I keep buying at regular intervals.

Another benefit of dollar cost averaging is that it helps you avoid letting emotion rule your stock purchases. It is completely natural for emotion to come into play when we are talking about investing. People panic when the markets are dropping because they have an instinctual fear of losing all their money. Of course, only in very rare instances does a company's stock drop all the way down, only to never recover. In 99.5% of cases, stocks recover after a major downturn, and over the long-term they end up being worth far more than they were even before the downturn in price.

Another way that emotion gets involved in investing is when people get too excited and greedy when they see stock prices moving up.

Dollar cost averaging helps you avoid all of this, because you simply make your purchases at pre-determined intervals and at specific amounts. This helps you avoid making foolish mistakes. Of course, it is going to take quite a bit of discipline in order to avoid falling prey to panic or greed. But when you see the market dropping, you need to recognize that as a buying opportunity. When you see the market going up, you need to recognize the fact that you are holding your investments over the long-term.

That is the third benefit of dollar cost averaging, in that it helps you stick to a long-term thinking pattern. What the markets to in response to the latest tweet or economic news is not going to matter in five years, much less ten or twenty.

Dollar cost averaging can also help you focus on bear markets. If you get the concept of dollar cost averaging and incorporate it into your way of thinking, then you will find yourself ready to start investing in shares when there are major downturns in the market. Let me advise you that you should prepare yourself now to make extra stock purchases when prices are dropping. You might even set aside some extra money for doing this. When everyone else is panicking, you can be purchasing more shares at discount prices. This will magnify the benefits of your dollar cost averaging program.

Let us use the Facebook example above to illustrate. Remember that we already got in a situation to buy more shares by following dollar cost averaging, and we ended up with 47 more shares which was an increase of about 15-16%. There were a couple of major downturns during the year, what if we had invested an extra $4200 during the biggest downturn? That could have gotten us an extra 33 shares. So, we could have finished the year out with 80 more shares, doing an extra buy during a downturn.

Downturns are actually a friend for the long-term investor, because we are interested in the trend that occurs over decades – and in most cases that is going to be up. But as dividend investors, we are more interested in getting regular dividend payments from more shares. So, if the market generally moves sideways in between now and retirement, that is not nearly as much of as an issue as it would be for a trader or someone who is hoping to build wealth from stock appreciation.

One complaint about dollar cost averaging is the more frequently you trade, the more costs you are going to rack up in brokerage commissions. But as we have seen, these days you can even sign up with commission free brokerages. So, the cost of making more frequent trades does not have to be an issue.

The main argument against dollar cost averaging is that in many cases, you are going to be buying shares of stock when the price is high. But as we have seen, the prices are going to average out, and this argument is dependent on the fallacy of being able to know the best time to buy and sell stocks. The fact is the day traders are full of it and that is why most of them lose money. It is not possible to know when stocks are going to rise or fall in price. Can you predict the next time the President is going to issue a tweet that will rattle the markets? No, you cannot – and you cannot predict a thousand other events that can cause prices to go up or down.

Diversification

The second important strategy that is used by long-term investors is diversification. This is the old do not put your eggs in one basket advice. The fact is, it continues to be good advice today.

Let US say that you own stock in the FAANGs, which is a slang term used on the markets for the leading tech companies. Generally speaking, this includes Facebook, Apple, Amazon, Netflix, and Google. However, this can include many other companies as well such as Twitter or SNAP.

Now suppose that Congress decided to investigate the FAANGs for privacy issues or even for monopoly powers. In fact, that is happening as I write this. If you had invested your entire portfolio in the five companies that make up this group, which is increasingly being targeted not only by Congress and the U.S. government but especially by the European Union, you might find yourself experiencing some investment pain.

For another example, suppose that you only invested in healthcare related companies. Suppose that Bernie Sanders or Elizabeth Warren wins the Presidency, and they get a Democratically controlled Congress as well. They might pass a Medicare for All bill that would completely eliminate private health insurance. As a practical matter, all of the companies you were invested in might have to find something else to do and they might even go out of business. At the very least, the passage of such a bill would probably mean their share prices would drop substantially, and so your investments would suffer a great deal.

These examples serve to illustrate that investing in just a few companies, especially if they are in the same sector, is not a good way to invest. While we used the example of government interference, there are many things that can impact individual companies or the sectors that they are in. So, it does not just include some major government action.

The bottom line is that putting all of your investments in a couple of healthcare companies, or just in Google and Amazon, would be a pretty bad idea. But you can balance out your portfolio by investing across different sectors and in multiple companies, and this will help protect you against the kind of issues that we described above.

Often, a related but different sector can benefit when one sector is having problems. If oil companies suddenly run into problems for one reason or another, natural gas or solar might be taking off. People will seek out alternative places to put their money when one sector runs into problems.

But human nature can rear it is ugly head here as well. People have their favorites among companies, and as you get to studying the financials of various companies and become familiar with their products and plans for the future, there is a good chance that you are going to be swooning for some of them. The danger of this is that you end up putting too much capital in a single investment. This is another example of the many ways that emotion can influence investment decisions, and this is not always for the best. Certainly, you can get excited about a single company, and investing in it might be a good idea. But you should have set rules about what percentage of your investment will go into a single company. And you should never exceed that rule.

We can always look back to see how companies performed in the past, but we do not know how they are going to perform in the future. There can be many factors that are going to influence the performance of the company as time goes on, and just like you can't know when a trend is really going to reverse with any level of acceptable accuracy, you are not going to be able to predict which companies are going to be around and successful ten or twenty years from now. So, the best thing is to spread out your investments among multiple companies. We can only tilt the odds in our favor, but we cannot control what is going to happen.

This brings us to the first major benefit that you will enjoy by setting up a diversified portfolio. We have been looking at dividend stocks and making estimates as to the amount of income that you could earn from them. However, a company's fortunes can go south at any time. Consider Abbvie, which we have repeatedly mentioned as a good investment. And it is a good investment right now, with a good dividend payment and a solid history.

But what if our government, which is leaning more toward the left and toward populism, brings either Medicare for all, price controls for prescription drugs, or both? This could really hurt the prospects of a pharmaceutical company like Abbvie. Their fortunes might take a major turn for the worse if both of these events happen, and they may not be able to maintain their dividend payments.

So, if you had invested all of your money in Abbvie, that could mean that you would be in trouble down the road. Not only could you see cuts in the dividend payment, the share price might drop substantially. That would mean that even if you sold your shares to get out and try and get into a better investment, you might end up with a lot less capital than you started out with.

The point of diversification is this for the dividend investor. If you have a solid, diversified portfolio, then you are not going to be dependent on just one stock for your income. If rather than composing 100% of your investments, or even 50%, Abbvie only makes up 5-10% of your overall portfolio, if it has bad fortunes in the future, you are still going to be able to survive, profit, and move on.

Remember that as a dividend investor, you are concerned about two major factors. These are the investment capital you used to buy the shares, and the stability or increase of the dividend payments. Diversification helps with both. In other words, you will be able to protect your capital by having a diversified portfolio because if you have 10 or 20 stocks, not all of them are going to go bad. Chances are that over the long term if you have chosen well, only a small fraction of your stocks are going to go bad. This means that by having a diversified portfolio you will be able to protect your investment capital.

Finally, some stocks are going to lose ground. Diversification is going to help protect you and minimize the risk of loss, because while some of your stocks are going to lose ground, others are going to gain ground. This is going to average out so that you aren't impacted very much by the losses. In fact, in some cases you are still going to come out ahead, because you may have been able to win big on some of your investments.

Now we need to think about what diversification is going to mean, when we are specifically considering dividend investing. People usually talk about diversification in general terms. For some hypothetical general investor, diversification is going to mean investing in some aggressive growth stocks, in some value stocks, in some bonds, and in some cash.

However, as a dividend investor we are not going to be looking at things quite in that way. So, we aren't looking to protect ourselves from the stock market per se, but rather from specific stocks that may run into trouble.

For us, diversification can take three forms. The first is that we are going to want to invest in a significant number of companies, so that no one company can control the fate of our portfolio. At a minimum, you should invest in ten companies. Twenty is far better, but it is going to take more work. Beyond twenty is probably going to end up being too much information to process. So, you should take a maximum of twenty-five companies.

Now you have a question of how much to put into each company. The best approach is to spread your investments fairly evenly. You should not put 50% or even 25% of your money into a single company.

There are many companies that look like they would be great for that, if you invested in them right now. That may hold true over the long term, but we have to say it again – you do not know what is going to happen over the long term. A company like Boeing or Disney might be a solid investment today, and it might be a solid investment in 30 years. But we simply have no idea what is going to happen between now and then. And in many cases, markets can be shaken up in their entirety. Companies that once held dominant positions can end up as former shadows of themselves.

So, it is best not to chance it by putting a large fraction of your investment capital in one company. There are many, many companies to choose from on the stock market that pay dividends. So, dividing up your investments among 10-20 good companies should not be a problem, and it should work out to provide a good income.

One problem with diversification when only buying individual stocks, is that you are going to end up at a point where you can't really keep track of them all very effectively. This is going to happen on two levels. You are going to have to keep track of your stocks for performance and monitoring their dividend payments and items like payout ratio. You are also going to want to keep up with the financials of the company. Unless you are able to work on this full-time, it is going to be difficult keeping track of more than a limited set of companies. You also might be interested in finding other companies to invest in.

As we will see in chapter 5, one way to get around this is to invest in dividend paying mutual funds or exchange traded funds. That is becoming an increasingly popular way to invest, and with good reason. Those types of investments will give you automatic exposure to tens, hundreds, and even thousands of companies through one investment and many funds pay good dividend payments. By investing some of your money in these types of funds, you will get massive diversification, and you will not be impacted by one or two companies going under at all. You can choose to include some funds as part of your overall portfolio, or you can even put all of your investments into funds.

As we will see in chapter 7, there are other ways to get dividend payments that do not involve buying stock in your typical large, publicly traded corporation. In that chapter we are going to talk about real estate investment trusts, master limited partnerships, and business development companies. These entities actually trade publicly on the major stock exchanges, but they give you the opportunity for exposure to a really diversified array of investments. This can help your portfolio stay strong and robust.

Now let us talk about sectors. When people think diversification, they might think of buying twenty stocks, but they might also be thinking of buying stock in Google, Facebook, Amazon, Apple….

In other words, they are thinking about buying a diversified portfolio of stocks, but they are thinking in terms of buying stocks in one sector. The example given above would be the high-tech sector. But in order to have a truly diversified portfolio, you need to be thinking more diversification than just buying different stocks. You also need to be thinking in terms of investing in different sectors of the economy.

In many cases, one sector of the economy can have a downturn. Or even in a major recession, some sectors are hurt more than others. Consider the 2008 crash which spread it is pain rather wide. Although everyone was affected, the banking and financial sector was hit particularly hard. So, you might imagine – if you had put all of your investments in the banking sector, you would have been worse off than if you had spread your investments across many sectors. Other sectors might have avoided dipping as low as the banking sector, and they may have recovered faster.

To summarize, a diversification plan should involve:

- Invest in at least 10-20 different dividend stocks.
- You should choose your investments from different sectors. Do not put all of your money into a single sector.
- Consider putting some of your investments in mutual funds or exchange traded funds that pay dividends. This can significantly reduce your risk by giving you large scale diversification. In this case, your only risk is the systemic risk that all investors face.
- Another option is to invest in alternative investments that generate income such as REITs.

Rebalancing

As time goes on, you are going to find that some parts of your investment portfolio grow faster than others. As a result, you might find that over time your investment portfolio is not bringing you closer to your goals. In order to bring it back into the kind of shape that you need it to be in, you might have to rebalance your portfolio. That can mean selling off some investments and then moving the money into other investments.

In most cases, people that use rebalancing are those who are using an investment portfolio with general classes of investments. Just say for example, you might have 25% of your total investment capital in cash and bonds. Then you might have 25% in safe dividend paying stocks, and 50% in aggressive growth stocks. At the end of the following year, you might find that the portion in aggressive growth stocks has grown a lot faster than the other parts of your portfolio. If the original distribution generally suits your investment goals and you do not want to increase your risk by having more of your money in aggressive growth stocks, then you might want to rebalance the portfolio.

Let us say that after a year now your portfolio has 60% in aggressive growth stocks, 20% in dividend paying stocks, and 20% in cash and bonds. In order to maintain the same balance, you would sell off some of the aggressive growth stocks. Then you would reinvest the profits in cash and bonds and dividend stocks to bring it back to a 50-25-25 balance.

The tendency of a portfolio to see more of it is weight go into one asset class versus another is called "portfolio drift". The goal with rebalancing is to keep risk in check, it is not to increase your returns. When you first create the asset, allocation used in your portfolio, this would have been done with your tolerance for risk and goals in mind. For some people, their asset allocation is going to be more conservative. Generally speaking, financial advisors think people should get more conservative as they age. Of course, this is one of those things that depends on the situation. The financial advisors are thinking of the ideal case, where someone graduates from college at age 23 and begins a perfect investment plan lasting over 30 or more years. Unfortunately, these days not many people are fitting that profile, which is why we have discussed the issue of older investors who need to play catch up. If you are in that situation, then moving to a conservative investment portfolio is not the best way to take care of things.

Of course, goals change with time, and you might find that the new arrangement is working better for you, when you have your sights set on new financial horizons. Some investors may decide that they need a more aggressive asset allocation than they thought they would need, and so they may decide to change direction.

As time goes on and your goals change, you should feel imprisoned by your prior asset allocation. You need to look at the trade-off between risk and returns on a periodic basis and see how things fit in with your changing life circumstances.

One of the questions that comes up is how often you should rebalance your portfolio. Some financial advisors suggest rebalancing your portfolio on a monthly basis, while others suggest a semi-annual or even annual time frame. This is a personal preference, but by and large an annual or once a year rebalancing is probably going to be best suited for most people. Over the course of a month, it is unlikely that a stock is going to take off that strongly, although that can happen at times. There also may be tax issues that can come up, by rebalancing once a year, you can minimize the impact of that.

Growth vs. Value Stocks

One issue that comes up when investors are looking for long-term strategies to use in the stock market, is whether to invest in growth or value stocks. First let us understand what the terms actually mean. A growth stock is one that gains value through capital appreciation over time. So, this is a stock where you are betting on stock prices increasing as the years and months go by. Investors that buy growth stocks are looking to get returns from future capital appreciation, and at some point, will sell off their stocks for a profit. Amazon is a good example of a growth stock, it is share prices have literally gone through the roof, it is now trading at around $1,900 a share. If you had bought Amazon 10 or 20 years ago, you are probably smiling at the thought.

Generally speaking, growth stocks are not going to be paying dividends. This goes back to our discussion in the first chapter – growth stocks are usually associated with companies that are themselves aggressively growing, trying to gain a lot more market share and move into more overseas markets. As we stated earlier, these types of companies are more likely to reinvest most or all of their profits into the growth of the company, whether that is in building new manufacturing plants, research and development, or hiring more employees or opening new stores.

As a result, most high-growth companies do not pay dividends. There are some that do, Apple is one of the best examples. However, Apple is also a high growth company. But if you check Apple's dividend payment, their yield is actually quite low. Personally, I would not be choosing Apple if I was looking for a dividend stock. Although the company does have a lot going for it, their yield is far too low to consider as an income stock.

Value stocks are basically stocks from solid companies that are undervalued, and what that means is their share price is lower than it should be. To determine if a stock is a value stock, you are going to want to look at the performance of the company. Share price is generally related to the performance of the company, such as earnings, profits, and so on. If a company has solid earnings, with revenue growth year-over-year, and it pays a good dividend, that should be a stock that is appealing to investors. Sometimes, there are many stocks that for whatever reason are ignored by the market. That means you can buy them at bargain prices. But it takes some work to find and identify value stocks.

Technically speaking, a stock does not have to pay dividends to be considered a value stock. The main thing with a value stock is that the stock itself is undervalued. That is the share price is too low, given the fundamentals of the company. The famous investor Warren Buffett is known to invest in value stocks.

The main thing to look for with a value stock is a low price to earnings ratio. So, this is going to be a company that has a good amount of earnings and profits, but it is going to have a low share price. A value stock will also have a low price to book ratio.

In order to determine whether or not a stock is a value stock, you are not going to be able to do it by just glancing at the price to earnings ratio. Nor are you going to be able to do it by looking at the stock price. What you have to do is compare the price to earnings ratio of this stock to similar companies. First off, you need to know the average price to earnings ratio for the stock market at large, but more importantly you need to know the price to earnings ratio for the sector that the company is in and compare it also to other companies that are in the same business.

So, you cannot determine if a stock is a value stock by comparing say, Apple to a utility company like Duke Energy. Not to use a pun, but that is an apples to oranges comparison. Also, you would not want to compare Facebook to United Health Care.

But you could compare Apple and Microsoft, or Facebook and Twitter. So, to use the pun again, compare apples to apples. If you are looking at pharmaceutical companies, for example, compare the company you are interested in to other pharmaceutical companies.

When it comes to stocks that pay dividends, one sign that you may be looking at a value stock, is that they are going to be paying a high yield. The yield is the dividend payment divided by the stock price. So, an undervalued company is going to have a low stock price, but the dividend payment may be consistent, and this will result in a high yield.

But a high yield by itself does not indicate that the stock is undervalued. You will have to cross check a high yield with the price to earnings ratio, and again compare to other similar companies in the same industry or sector. You might also want to compare the yield to other companies that are in the same sector.

Value stocks represent an opportunity for investors. The main reason is that you are going to have a chance to get into stocks at bargain prices. For those who are short-term traders or looking to profit from appreciation of share price, value stocks might be a bit of a risk. This is because the stock price might not appreciate and then the investor will not be able to turn a profit on their shares. But as a dividend investor, these issues are not a concern. You are going to find value stocks of interest because you will be able to get into a value stock at a low price and enjoy the high yields paid on the dividends. That means to attain a given amount of income, you will have to buy fewer shares of stock than you otherwise would have.

Others see value stocks as an opportunity, because at some point, if the company keeps performing well, the market is going to recognize this. That means that down the road the share price is going to rise.

Dividend investors tend to be interested in value stocks because these are often mature companies that pay regular dividends.

To summarize, a value stock is going to have the following characteristics:
- Company fundamentals, like earnings and profits will be solid.
- It will have a low price to earnings ratio and a low price to book ratio. You will want to compare the price to earnings ratio to other similar companies in the same industry and the same sector. If the company is in the

S & P 500, or some other index, find out what the average price to earnings ratio is for the index. Then compare that to the company. If the company has a low P/E ratio compared to the index, that is an indication that it is a value stock. Keep in mind that sometimes, an entire sector may be undervalued. So, it is helpful to check against the index besides looking at similar companies.

- If the company pays dividends, a value stock is going to have a high yield when compared against it is peers.

When to Get Out of an Investment

Over time, some of the investment opportunities that you were thrilled about are not going to work out. If you have chosen well, most will remain stable and will probably pay good dividends. However, some companies are going to fade from the scene, that is just a fact of life. You might find that the company is unable to continue paying the level of dividend payments that you were seeking. Or the company's share might tank for one reason or another. It might be pushed out of a market, or even be forced into bankruptcy. Many once solid companies have gotten into big trouble and even gone out of business. Consider Lumber Liquidators, whose share dropped to completely worthless after a scandal involving chemicals in their wood flooring hit the news media. GM went very close to bankruptcy, and it is shares became worthless as a result. Another example is Bear-Sterns, which was a 100-year-old investment bank that had been considered to be a rock-solid investment. It went belly up during the financial crisis in 2008 when plunging mortgage securities wiped out the company's value.

So, there are no guarantees that an investment today is going to be there for you tomorrow. That is why diversification is so important. With significant diversification of your portfolio, one GM or Bear-Sterns is not going to wipe you out.

The key is knowing when to get out. First off, you will need to pay attention to the news surrounding a company. The best-case scenario is getting out before the stock price takes a nosedive, so that you can recoup your initial investment and then put that money into another company that pays dividends.

If catastrophic news about a company that you have invested in hits the media, this is probably a situation where you are going to want to reconsider your investments. Of course, you are want to going to use careful and reasoned logic when evaluating the situation. Do not panic every time there is bad news about a company. Often bad news comes out, but it only impacts the company for a short time period.

In most cases, when we are talking about getting out of dividend paying stocks, we are going to be thinking about a situation where over a long period of time, the share price of the stock is gradually declining, and/or they are paying lower dividend payments. You should evaluate the health of your investments on an annual basis. So, in addition to doing rebalancing at the beginning of each year, you should take a look at each one of your individual investments to check it is performance and see if the stock continues to look solid.

If you start spotting problems, then it might be time to get out of the stock. You might have another stock that is looking much better, and it could be a good idea to get out of the stock that is languishing or in decline and move your money into the new investment.

Keep in mind you do not have to completely abandon a stock that looks like it is heading for trouble all at once. You can take an approach of gradually reducing your exposure. For example, you could move out 25% of your investment from the troublesome stock either to new investments or to existing ones that look better. Then a few months later (one quarter say), re-evaluate the situation. Maybe the company will start showing signs of a turn around. If it is still having troubles, you can get out completely at that point, or you can continue your gradual approach. You could sell off another 25% and then let another quarter go by, in order to see if the company improved it is fortunes, and in that case, you might want to stay in the investment.

Sometimes, you might have some companies in your portfolio that are doing OK, but they have not turned out to be that great or you might come across a company that seems like a better dividend investment. This could be a case where moving your money from one investment to another would be a wise decision.

In all of these cases, you are going to want to consider your fundamental analysis. If a company underperforms over several successive quarters, this can hurt the stock price significantly, and that might be a good reason to get out of the stock. Watching the dividend payout ratio could be important as well. If the company's earnings are not keeping up, but the company is paying a high dividend such that the payout ratio goes over 100%, this can be a red flag. This is not an issue that calls for knee jerk reactions. You do not want to automatically abandon ship when you see the payout ratio has increased. However, it does call for more investigation. You will want to look closely at the company's fundamentals, as well as it is future plans. In chapter 8 we will discuss many of the issues that you should be considering when doing fundamental analysis.

Remember that when it comes to investing, we are all weakened by the fact that we have imperfect information at our fingertips. One of the problems is that we cannot know the future. We can only make reasonable estimates about the future.

So, there are going to be times when you make mistakes. A company might look like it was going headfirst into the dirt, and so you might get out of your investment. Then in a couple of years, you might find that the company is doing well, and you will regret having got out of it. Then you will be filling your mind with "what if?" scenarios, related to how well you would have done if only you had stayed in the company.

But you cannot approach investing in this way. You have to focus on the good items in your portfolio instead, and not worry about supposed lost opportunities. Keep in mind that it will be better to prematurely get out of an investment that looked like it was going bad, than to hold onto the investment far too long and end up losing a large amount of money.

Simply Have a Plan,

It may sound a bit ridiculous, but you would be surprised at how many people invest in the stock market without giving it much thought. A lot of them do it based on good instincts. So, the fact that you simply are developing a plan to direct your investing, is something that is going to put you above 90% of the people that are involved in the stock market.

Chapter 5: Earning Dividend Income From Mutual Funds and Exchange Traded Funds

In the last chapter, we harped on the importance of diversification. Any financial advisor that you are going to talk to is going to emphasize the importance of a diversified portfolio when it comes to investing. However, really diversifying your investments is quite difficult as an individual investor. It is difficult to get enough companies into your portfolio while also thoroughly evaluating their fundamentals while also keeping track of them once you have sunk money into them. It is also difficult for an individual investor to get enough money into each company to really get good dividend payments.

One way around some of these issues is to put your money into funds that pay out dividends. This can help you get exposure to hundreds, and even thousands of companies. You can also get wide exposure to many sectors and industries by investing in the appropriate funds.

For some investors, this is the way to go, without bothering investing in individual stocks. For others, you may only be interested in individual stocks and find the idea of investing in funds boring. Many investors can do a combination of both, however, and that is the power of this concept. Instead of investing in 20 different stocks, you can invest in 5-10 of your favorite stocks and then put the rest of your investment capital in a few different dividend paying funds that give you highly diversified exposure.

What is a Mutual Fund

A mutual fund is a pooled amount of money collected from investors that is used to buy shares of stock or other investments. The pool of money that is collected is divided up into shares in it is own right (these are sometimes called units in the case of mutual funds). The shares are then sold to investors, so the investors own an interest in the underlying shares of stock or other securities, but the company that runs the fund is the actual owner of the securities that underlie the fund.

A mutual fund is going to invest in a large number of different assets. So, it might invest in 50 or 100 different stocks, or even more. Many mutual funds track major stock indexes, such as the S & P 500, the Russell 2000, or the Dow Jones Industrial Average. So, a fund that tracked the S & P 500 would own shares in all 500 companies that make up the index. In the case of the Russell 2000, the fund would own stock in 2000 companies.

This provides a great deal of diversification, to a level that simply is not possible for most individual investors. Without a billion dollars to throw around, you aren't going to be able to buy shares in all of the 2000 companies that make up the Russell 2000, or even the 500 companies that make up the S & P 500.

However, a mutual fund gives you exposure to these diversified investments. So, you can enjoy the benefits of massive diversification, in a way that hedges possible losses. If one or two, or even five of the companies on the S & P 500 went under, it would not affect you that much if the rest of the economy was on solid footing. But on the other hand, with an investment that broad in major companies, you can take full advantage of the growth that the stock market has to offer. We are also going to see that you can get dividend payments from investments in mutual funds (and also exchange traded funds).

The Benefits of Mutual Fund Investing

In 2018, and amazing amount of money - $19 trillion to be exact – was invested in mutual funds. We have already seen one of the benefits of investing in mutual funds, you get massive diversification. If one company in a mutual fund fails or runs into problems, that is probably going to be offset by gains among other companies in the fund. So, your exposure to risk is quite limited. Remember that there is always systemic risk. Even investing in a mutual fund may not protect you from systemic risk, if the economy goes down it is also going to take mutual funds down with it. However, it does minimize un-systemic risk.

Mutual funds allow you to get diverse exposure to a large number of companies with the convenience of being able to make relatively small investments. Many mutual funds do have minimum investment requirements. Some investment funds might have a minimum requirement of $500, but others might have an investment requirement as high as $5,000. This is something to consider, but as we will see later, exchange traded funds get around this type of requirement, and so for many investors offer a better route to use to get the same benefits.

Many investors like mutual funds because it is a form of passive investing. That is, when you invest in mutual funds, you are not going to have any active role to play other than deciding if you want to get out of the fund or buying more shares. You are not going to have to study any company fundamentals or anything like that. Many readers are not going to be interested in this approach, because if you are looking to build a self-managed portfolio you might be really interested in the idea of investigating companies and stock picking. That sort of thing does not go on with mutual funds.

Different funds have different investment goals. This is one reason that many investors find mutual funds appealing. So, if you are looking for aggressive growth, you can find a mutual fund that is specifically designed for that purpose. You can also look for high dividend yield investments. There are also value stock mutual funds that can be invested in. You can buy into mutual funds that are designed to protect your capital, or other mutual funds designed to generate rapid growth.

Mutual funds have a professional fund manager that does all the fund management on your behalf. So, with the goals of the fund in mind, the fund manager is going to buy and sell shares of stock that they believe will keep the performance of the fund at a high level. Typically, the goal is to beat some market index. If you are investing but your investments are beating the S & P 500, for example, then you know you have a good investment. That might be hard for an individual investor to pull off, but the idea of a professional fund manager is actually a little bit controversial. The controversy swirls around the idea of whether or not the money manager actually provides significant benefit, or whether they provide benefit at all. The presence of the fund manager is not a trivial issue, as it costs a lot of money. The costs of this are accounted for in the many fees that you have to pay in order to stay invested in the mutual fund.

Classes of Mutual Funds

There are four general classes or types of mutual funds. The first type of mutual fund is for investment in stocks. Sometimes these are called equity funds. Within this class of mutual fund, there are several types that are generally based on the goal of the investments. For example, as a dividend investor you are probably going to be interested in an equity fund that is also an income fund. This is going to be a mutual fund that invests in a large number of stocks that pay dividends, and then the fund will divided up the dividends and pay them out on a per share basis. This is done on the number of shares or units in the mutual fund. So, the fund will receive the dividend payments from all of it is stocks, and then it divides that value by the total number of shares in the mutual fund. Then you are paid an amount proportional to the number of shares you own.

There are also growth funds, and sector funds that are available. As we noted above, many large mutual funds also track major stock indices like the S & P 500. More than half of all mutual funds are equity funds.

You can also invest in fixed-income mutual funds. This should not be confused with income funds that are based on stocks that pay dividends. Fixed-income funds are mutual funds that invest in bonds. There can be a wide variation among these, as some bond funds will be focused on government bonds and others will be focused on corporate bonds. A bond is a loan that investors make to the government or corporation, although people do not tend to view it that way (they see it as an investment). So just like a regular loan, a bond pays interest payments and it has a maturity date when your principal is returned. Unlike the types of loans an individual would take out, the company or government entity only makes interest payments, and they do not make dated payments on the principal, they keep it until the end of the term for the bond.

Aggressive growth funds invest in stocks, but they focus on rapidly growing small cap companies and startups. Some aggressive growth funds also invest in rising companies in developing markets that a high potential for large amounts of growth. These funds are viewed as having high risk. They can drop by large amounts as well as grow by large amounts.

Mutual funds are also available as "balanced funds" that can be put together in different mixtures in order to meet different investment goals. Balanced funds will invest some of their money in stocks, and some in bonds, and some in other types of financial securities.

Finally, there are money market funds. These are very low risk investments that focus on low risk bonds like U.S. treasuries.

Costs and fees

One of the biggest problems with mutual funds is that there are many costs associated with them. You will have to weigh whether or not the costs make investing in mutual funds worth it. When you are looking to get dividend income from your mutual fund investments, the fees and commissions might be troublesome. Frankly it may not be worth it.

The first term that you are going to hear thrown around when it comes to mutual funds is the load. There are mutual funds that are load, and there are no-load mutual funds.

A load is a sales commission. There are different ways that loads are charged. A front-end load is one that is charged when you put money in to invest. These fees are deducted from the amount of money you invest, so if you put in $500, and there is a 6% front-end load, which is $30. So, when you invest $500, you are actually only investing $470, after the fees are taken out. The purpose of these fees is to pay the professional money manager that manages the fund.

A back-end load, also called a contingent deferred sales charge, is a fee that is charged when you take money out of the investment account.

No-load funds do not have fund managers. So, there is no commission, or load, charged when investing or pulling money out of a no-load mutual fund. But they do have other fees associated with them, so you are still going to have to pay money for the mutual fund that could cut into your earnings.

There are other fees that may be associated with a mutual fund. For example, they may charge an asset under management fee, if they have a fund manager. The fee is going to be a percentage of the amount of money that is in your account. So, the more money you accumulate in your account, the more the fees.

You will also have to pay another fee called an expense ratio. This is another fee that is charged as a percentage of your total investment. The purpose of the expense ratio is to cover the costs of the company running the fund. Costs are broken down into management fees, distribution and service fees, and administrative fees. Management fees cover the management of the fund, that is this is money to pay the people who are buying and selling shares in the fund. Distribution and service fees actually cover advertising and marketing expenses used to promote the mutual fund to other potential investors.

Mutual Funds that Pay Dividends

There are many mutual funds that invest in dividends, offered by a wide array of companies. This allows you to get a diversified investment portfolio while also receiving dividend income. Note that when you receive dividends from a mutual fund, they are unqualified. That means that you are going to have to treat the income from dividend payments coming out of mutual funds as ordinary income, and it will be taxed at ordinary income tax rates, rather than at capital gains rates.

Let us take a look at a couple of examples. One fund that pays dividends I the DRIPX fund. It invests in companies that have DRIPS, which as you may recall are dividend reinvestment plans. So, the dividends earned by the fund are going to be reinvested. The yield is 1.75% and the ten-year return was 13%.

VIHIX is the Vanguard International High Dividend Yield Index Fund. This fund invests in international companies and seeks to generate income. It is looking for high dividend yields from companies that are growing slowly. It will provide current income. This fund has a respectable 4% yield, and a low expense ratio.

Mutual Funds – The bottom line

For those who want someone else to manage their investments, mutual funds might be an option to consider. However, if you are reading this book then chances are you are looking to take a more active role in your investing. Even if you are inclined to take the mutual fund route, a good piece of advice is not to do so. You can get most of the same benefits from exchange traded funds, with the exception of having a professional fund manager. It is not clear that a professional fund manager is really a benefit. For one, it is not really clear that they actually beat the market any better than a passively managed fund like an exchange traded fund. Also, you have to pay all the expenses associated with the loads and fees. You should think about dividend investing as going into business for yourself. With that in mind, you are going to want to minimize your expenses to the fullest extent possible. So why pay huge load fees when you do not have to?

Another thing that has to be considered is that when looking at a lot of mutual funds, they often have pretty low yields compared to individual stocks that you might pick. That reduces the appeal.

There is no point paying expenses that you do not have to pay, when there is not really a compelling argument in their favor. The real argument in favor of mutual funds is being able to get a high level of diversification. Another argument in their favor is being able to invest in funds that will specifically match your investment goals. However, as we are about to see, we can get these advantages from mutual funds without the downsides by investing in exchange traded funds.

What is an Exchange Traded Fund?

An exchange traded fund can be thought of as a mutual fund that trades on a stock exchange and exists without a fund manager. An exchange traded fund still has to be managed, as the company that runs them still has to buy and sell the stocks and so forth, but the expense ratios for exchange traded funds tend to be minimal. Exchange traded funds do not charge loads or other fees, and you can buy and sell them at will on the stock exchanges. So, while many mutual funds are going to have minimum investment requirements that could be $5,000, exchange traded funds do not have official minimum investment requirements. So, the minimum investment requirement is going to be the price of buying one share of stock.

Exchange traded funds are also available to meet any investment need. The growth of exchange traded funds over the past 20 years has been explosive, and so you are going to be able to find a fund to meet any investment goal, including buying into funds that pay dividends. They are also offered by a wide array of different companies, and so you will be able to find exchange traded funds that have different costs of entry – that is you can invest in different funds that have the same stated goal, but that may have different share prices, making it easier for you to invest. You can also review each fund for it is performance metrics, to see how the return on the fund has been historically, in addition to looking for funds that pay dividends.

So, when you think about it, exchange traded funds are like mutual funds but without all the baggage. One thing that we did not mention with mutual funds is that they only trade once per day after market close. So, you can go to your mutual fund company and place an order for more shares in the fund, and this will be taken care of in the evening. However, with exchange traded funds they are live on the stock market and so you are going to be able to buy and sell shares as you wish just like any other stock.

How do Dividend ETFs work?

An exchange traded fund that pays out dividends is one that invests in multiple dividend paying stocks. The fund will collect the dividend payments from individual stocks and pull them together into a large dividend fund which it then distributes to the investors in the exchange traded fund in proportion to the number of shares owned by each investor. Keep in mind that not all exchange traded funds are going to pay out cash from dividends. The funds manager can decide whether or not the dividends are actually paid out or if they are reinvested. So, when selecting a dividend exchange traded fund this is going to be something that you are going to want to research to make sure that you get exactly what you're expecting.

Since exchange traded funds have to collect dividends from the stocks that the fund holds, if the fund pays dividends out as cash, this is going to happen at a later date. But since exchange traded funds or treated like stocks, they are going to have similar deadlines that stocks do which pay dividends.

That means that in exchange traded fund is going to have an ex-dividend date and a date of record which function just like they would for regular stock offered by companies. In other words, these dates are used in order to determine which investors are eligible to receive the dividend payments. Each exchange traded fund that pays dividends we'll also have a payment date associated with the dividend.

Just like a company, an exchange traded fund will have a prospectus for investors. If there are funds that you are interested in, you can get a copy of the prospectus online and read the prospectus to find out when these dates typically occur.

Typically exchange traded funds which pay out cash for dividends are going to collect the money from the dividends they receive the other stocks fund is invested in, and it will put that money in a non-interest-bearing account. The monies put into the account to hold it until the fund has collected all the dividends it is due to receive. Then it holds them until it is own payment date when it divides up the money proportionately depending on how many shares you hold in the fund, and then it pays out the cash.

Some funds actually handle this differently. Rather than putting the money into a holding account, they will temporarily invest the funds into additional shares of stock. Then when the payment date arrives, they will sell those shares in order to get the cash needed to pay out the dividends to the investors. Otherwise the money is distributed in the same way, that is each investor in the fund is going to receive a payment amount proportional to the number of shares that they own.

Cash or Reinvestment?

Whether or not you choose to receive cash payments, or you would prefer that your dividends be reinvested, something to consider is that having the dividends reinvested on your behalf could be an important growth strategy before retirement. Many exchange traded funds have very high annual returns. What does this mean for the individual dividend investor? Essentially it means that Exchange traded funds that automatically reinvest the money could serve as a high-growth investment to use in order to prepare yourself for the future. So, while that particular fund may not provide dividend income now, what it could do is help you grow your overall base of capital that can be used for investments. So after taking advantage of the high growth capabilities of some of these funds compounded by having your dividend payments reinvested, later on you could sell off the shares and then use the proceeds to invest in stocks that you will use to actually receive cash payments at retirement.

Example Funds

Exchange traded funds that pay dividends are offered by a wide variety of companies. Vanguard is one of the most famous mutual fund companies that also offers a wide range of exchange traded funds that you can invest in. One of the exchange traded funds of interest that they offer is called the Vanguard high dividend yield ETF. The ticker is VYM. However, it actually only pays $1 per share annually, and the yield is a mere 0.56%. One reason that you might invest in the fund anyway is to take advantage of capital appreciation.

Now let us take a look at the fun called SDY which is a fund that attracts the Standard and Poors aristocrat index. These are stocks that have been paying increasing dividends for at least 20 years. The funds yield is better then V YM, however it is still not that impressive at 2.38%. But one thing to note about this fund is that the year to date return at the time of writing is 12.47%. That is a really high return. As they say past performance is not a guarantee of future success. However, outside of recessions it is reasonable to assume that the return will continue to be in the same ballpark. So, this is an example of a fun that would be useful for those who need to grow the size of their portfolio because they were lacking in investment until now. Another advantage with this fund besides the high year-to-date return, is the fact that it only trades add a little bit less than $100 per share. So, it would not be super difficult to build up a significant investment in the fund.

Another interesting fund is the iShares DVY. This fund also trades and a bit under $100 per share. But it has even better characteristics with a year-to-date return a 15.5%. In addition, it pays a respectable yield of 3.38%. This fund actually tracks smaller companies that pay dividends. It also includes many investments in utility companies. The fund is highly diverse however, so that's why he has a high growth rate which could seem a little bit surprising given that utility companies are not exactly high-growth opportunities.

A similar fund is run by Vanguard and offered under the ticker VIG. This fund has a lower yield at 1.75%. However, it has a surprising year-to-date return of 20.51%. Another example of a high return which could make these funds extremely valuable for those who need to grow their capital rather quickly. This actually seems to be a low risk way to accomplish that goal.

Exchange Traded Funds for Dividends – the Bottom Line

If you do a lot of research, chances are you are going to be able to find a lot of stocks that pay higher yields then those typically seen with exchange traded funds. However, it is important to keep in mind that there are some trade-offs that must be considered here. The first of those trade-offs is that exchange traded funds centered on dividend paying stocks tend to have surprisingly high returns. Therefore, as we stated earlier, it is probably going to be the case that these funds are not of interest to people that are looking to build a portfolio to live on. The low yields translate into relatively low dividend payments per share. If you are looking to live on dividend payments, then you need to be looking at cash. And the amount of cash paid out per-share is going to be the important metric in that case. So those people who are ready to live on a dividend income right now, are generally probably not going to be interested in using many of these exchange traded funds in order to generate income.

But as we said earlier, many investors who are over 45 or 50, have not been building up an investment account. So, if you find yourself in that situation a year-to-date return which is gains in the stock price, is something that seriously needs to be considered. The reader who is paying attention would have noticed that all of these exchange traded funds that we examined had high year to date returns.

Of course, not all of them do, but there are so many that do it is not hard to find one. In fact, these are some of the best investments around. Is just generally difficult to get an investment that is going to give you a 20% return within a year. So those of you who are off to a late start investing should consider these vehicles as a way to grow your investment portfolio rapidly. The same advice holds that we would say for anything else. So, you do not want to pick one of these funds and then throw all of your money into it. What you need to do is use the same procedure and get some diversity in your investments. That is, you want to invest in multiple ETFs, just in case some of them do not work out.

With the ETFs however, the risk is going to be mostly systemic. So that means these types of funds are sensitive to large-scale or gross features of the economy in the world situation. Therefore, if the economy goes down, the value of these funds is going to go down as well. But remember that recessions are short-lived. In the vast majority of cases, recessions are over in a year or two, and stocks quickly regain their past values. So, if you were to invest in some funds like this in order to grow wealth overtime, the last thing that you want to do is to panic whenever there is a market downturn. You should write it out and go for the long-term gains that you are likely to see from these types of investments.

So, what are the advantages of exchange traded funds. The first advantage is that they offer Extreme levels of diversification. So, if you're looking to get some of that into your portfolio this could be one way to do it. However, some readers are going to find that the low yields relatively speaking, are not high enough to justify the investment. That is going to be something that you have to look into on your own.

The second advantage of exchange traded funds is the high year-to-date returns that you are going to see with many versions of these funds. These returns are so high that they are pretty much unmatched anywhere else.

Now the next advantage that we are going to discuss is the low expense ratio. So, this is not an advantage that an exchange traded fund has in relation to the money that you might invest in individual stocks. However, the low fees related to exchange traded funds is a huge advantage when they are compared against mutual funds. Consider the fund SPY. This fund tracks the S&P 500 index. It is year-to-date return is an extremely high 18.51%. Returning to the topic at hand, expense ratio is only 0.09%. Exchange traded funds bark passively managed and so they are saddled with commissions and fees the way that mutual funds are.

Whether or not Exchange traded funds are better than mutual funds, is going to be a matter of taste and probably your personality type. Those who are more active in their approach to investing are definitely going to find that they prefer exchange traded funds. The reason is that since they trade like stocks, even though they offer you a protected index fund type of investing, they will involve active investing and trading decisions. So, this is little bit different from mutual funds. You are going to have a professional fund manager. Also, you can actively trade them during the day which is not something you can do with mutual funds.

But the biggest advantage over mutual funds is the low expense ratio combined with the fact that there are no loads (or commissions).

The Final Recommendation

So, let us cut to the chase. If you are looking to build a dividend income, Exchange traded funds are not something that I would recommend as your main goal in getting this income. The reason is simple, and that is the low yields that these funds tend to pay. The yields are so low in most cases, that it would require that you purchase a huge number of shares in order to realize the kind of income goals that you may have. If you are middle class dividend investor, you probably are not going to be able to put together a portfolio based on Financial securities that pay 2% or less when it comes to yield. The fact is you are going to be able to find many stocks that pay much higher yields. We could be talking about two times or three times the yield seen here.

That said, the extremely high returns that these funds have seen is not something to dismiss. So, as we have said multiple times already, those readers who have not been investing perhaps at all or at least a not significant amounts, should be attracted to the extremely high year-to-date returns that we have seen with some of these investments. So that means that we can kind of think of these funds as a bailout tool that can help turn things around with the 20% or thereabouts annual returns that these funds can provide. Of course, you have to remember the disclaimer about stocks that past performance is not a guarantee of future results. So, although these funds have done extremely well in the past, that does not necessarily mean that they are going to continue doing so. But that is a risk that you take with any investment.

Now let us turn our attention to mutual funds specifically. Personally, I am not a big fan of them. They are designed for passive investors, and that is the first thing that you want take into consideration. But the main thing to worry about with mutual fund investing, is the fees. If you do decide to get into mutual fund investing, at the very least you should seek out no load mutual funds. There is no sense eating into your profits by paying loads, and other expensive fees in order to fat my wallet of some money manager.

But our general recommendation is to avoid Mutual funds unless you are not planning to be a dividend investor.

Chapter 6: Explode Your IRA

In this chapter we are going to shift gears a little bit and look at the issue of the individual retirement accounts, or as they are often commonly known, IRA's. An individual retirement account is something that individually directed investors can use for one reason or another. It may be the case that they were originally created for the sole purpose of helping self-employed people and others build a retirement account when they weren't working at a large company. So basically, an IRA can take the form of something to replace a 401(k) that you may be offered at your place of employment. However, many people use them as an adjunct account.

But one of the problems with IRAs, is that you are very limited with regard to the amount of money that you can invest. First of all, since this is an individual account, there is not going to be any employer matching. The employee contribution limit for a 401(k) is about $19,000 per year. However, for an IRA it is only $5,500 if you are under the age of 50, and $6,500 if you are over the age of 50.

Why you should use dividends to grow your IRA

These strict contribution limits mean that an IRA is not something that is going to launch you into the stratosphere of wealth. However, using dividends, you can grow your IRA even more rapidly. It is actually pretty easy to do.

Many people who have IRA's may not be thinking in terms of investing in dividend stocks. However, this can be a large mistake. There are a couple of ways that dividend payments from stocks that are inside your IRA can help you.

First let us consider dividend earning investments. You can buy stocks inside your IRA that pay dividends. Each quarter, they are going to be sending you payments. But these payments are going to remain inside your individual retirement account. The dividend payments that you earn will accumulate in the account, and this can create a growing cash balance.

This cash balance from your dividend payments is something that you can use to get around the normal contribution limits. Of course, you cannot take it out of your account without paying a tax penalty anyway. So, you can use the accumulated dividend payments in order to buy more stocks inside your IRA account. In short, this is a situation that works as if you had contributed more money into your account. Consider investing in some stocks that have high dividend payments, that way you will make progress faster. It will be as if Congress changed the law and was now allowing you to deposit even more money into your IRA.

Dividend Election

You have two choices. You can take cash for dividend payments or elect to reinvest the dividends. Prior to retirement, you are not going to pull out the cash unless you have come into some kind of emergency, so the only issue here is whether or not you want to have direct control of the cash and choose where to reinvest it yourself, or whether you want this process to happen automatically, which is going to mean that the dividend payments you receive are going to be reinvested in the stocks that you already hold. Either way, contact your broker, or the mutual fund company if you have a mutual fund for this purpose, and tell them what dividend election you want to use. You can either select reinvest or cash. If you choose cash, be sure to invest the cash you get into new stock purchases.

Withdrawals of Dividends

If you are earning dividend income that you are taking as cash, and it is taken out of your IRA, you are not going to benefit from any capital gains taxes. In the case of an IRA, dividend payments are going to be considered to be regular withdrawals from your individual retirement account. If you have a traditional IRA, that means that you are going to be taxed on the dividend payments as if they were ordinary income. However, for those with a Roth IRA, there could be huge advantages. The money will have grown tax free in your account over the years, and you will be able to withdraw the money as regular withdrawals from your Roth IRA, which means that they could be tax free.

Note that if you take money out of an IRA before age 59 ½, you will incur a 10% tax penalty, in addition to any income tax that you may owe on the income.

How withdrawals work in practice

Besides the tax implications, you might be wondering how you can pull out the cash after retirement when you are getting regular dividend payments. Most brokerages allow you to setup regular cash payments of your dividend earnings every quarter. These withdrawals can be set up to operate on an automatic basis. Check with your brokerage for details.

Chapter 7: Nontraditional Sources of Income

Up until this point in the book, we have talked about receiving dividend payments from corporations that are publicly traded on the stock exchanges. We are going to continue talking about publicly traded companies, but it turns out that there are a large number of companies that are not regular corporations that pay out dividends. There are three special classes of companies that are setup with the express purpose of paying out their profits to investors. These are specialized companies that are in three sectors – real estate, energy, and investment. These companies often offer high yields with low share prices, and so you will find that they are an opportunity to build up your dividend portfolio without having to put up as much capital. Many of them are also involved in solid sectors of the economy that are usually good to invest in. Of course, the same rules apply here that apply elsewhere, you would not want to put all of your money down to your last dime that you can invest into the tech sector. And, you are not going to want to do that here either. For example, many of the companies that we are going to discuss below are energy companies involved in oil and gas. It is entirely possible that the oil and gas sectors could suffer an economic downturn, that often happens. Maybe for some companies, the oil is going to dry up. So that could mean that your investments in these companies could go belly up.

The bottom line is you do not want to pick one of these companies and see that it pays a high dividend, and then put all of your investment capital into that single company where something bad can happen and wipe you out. But as a part of a larger and diverse portfolio, you can definitely sink significant capital in the investments that were are going to discuss in this chapter.

Reits

The first type of investment that we are going to consider covers a lot of ground. This is a type of company that is called a real estate investment trust. As you are going to see in a moment, some of the things that are considered "real estate" are a bit surprising.

However, REITs also allow you to invest in conventional real estate. This real estate can take the form of commercial office space, rental homes, or apartments. Many large investment companies got involved in home rental when the housing market collapsed in 2008. You can invest in these types of companies in order to receive regular dividends out of the payment streams that these companies collect from their renters.

In addition to rental homes, many of these companies also invest in apartment buildings, or structures like duplexes. Although some people are deadbeat renters, that is usually short-lived, and most renters pay their rent on time on a regular basis. That means that the companies that are renting these buildings are collecting monthly payments, and so they are cash rich and able to pay out their dividend payments.

In fact, a real estate trust is a special setup that was created by Congress in the early 1960s. The trust must pay out 90% of the income that comes in to investors. The trust has a partner that manages it, and they are entitled to taking 10% of the money.

What is interesting about REITs, is that while they include what you think of when you hear the word real estate, there are many different kinds of real estate trusts. This is one of the most diverse sectors you can think of, and you could built up a diverse portfolio only considering these companies.

Let us consider something you are probably very familiar with. That is hotels and motels. While you may know the Marriot, Holiday Inn, and other famous hotels and motels, what you may not be aware of is that most of these companies actually rent the buildings that they are using for the hotel. How crazy is that?

So, guess what? There are real estate trusts that own and manage these properties. And more to the point, you can invest in these real estate trusts and earn dividends. Again, this is an evergreen investment, just like houses and apartments. People are always going to need a place to live. The fortunes of rental homes may go up and down somewhat, but there is always a steady stream of people that are interested in renting a home.

Another thing to consider is that people are always going to be traveling. The level of travel may go up and down somewhat, and we are not saying that these companies are immune to a downturn that could severely impact the travel sector. However, it is unlikely that such a downturn would be completely catastrophic. Chances are good that these types of investments are pretty safe as far as investing goes.

Another well-known type of real estate trust are those that manage office buildings and shopping malls. These can also provide sustained income, but of the REITs that we have thought about so far, those that manage shopping malls might be the ones that are at the highest level of risk at the present time.

Office buildings, generally speaking, are probably more sustainable. Of course, the economy is going to go through ups and downs, but office buildings, over time, are going to be mostly rented out. And once again, this is another situation where you benefit from the steady stream of rental income provided to the management company.

Remember that if someone gets evicted for not paying their rent, a new renter is not far behind.

From here, the types of investments that are available in the form of real estate trusts begins to become a little bit exotic. Let us start with cell phone towers. It might seem strange, but cell phone towers are considered as real estate. And again, although you might think of the big carriers as owning the towers, it is actually real estate trusts that own cell phone towers, and they are leased to communications companies like Verizon. There is not any possibility that I can see that smart phones are going anywhere, and so it is reasonable to assume that investing in companies that manage cell phone towers is a pretty good investment for the near future.

For another surprise, consider cloud computing. You have probably heard about companies like Facebook, Amazon, and Microsoft getting into cloud computing. In fact, many companies are getting on board with cloud computing, because they need it to store the huge amounts of data that they are collecting, and many of these companies are running the data through machine learning systems in order to extract useful information out of it.

By now, you should not be surprised at what real estate trusts can offer.

So, you will not be too shocked to learn that many real estate trusts own banks of computers in chilled buildings that are leased out for cloud computing purposes. This is a type of real estate trust, cell phone towers being another, that is strongly oriented toward the future economy. That means these are very good investments, and they are likely to be very robust over the long term.

The only downside with REITS is that the income you receive from the dividends paid on them does not qualify for capital gains tax rates. The income from REITs is considered as regular or ordinary income.

Master Limited Partnerships

Now we are going to change gears and talk about another special structure that Congress setup which is a master limited partnership. In this type of business, you are actually a "limited partner" in the company. The way that you become a partner is by purchasing shares in the company. The company is managed by a "general partner", that actually runs the business. They take a share of the profits for their troubles; it is usually around 10%.

Those who are limited partners are paid dividends for their investment. This works in some respects the same way that dividend payments from REITs work. That is, they are not treated as qualified dividends. That means that the income you generate from these types of companies cannot be considered capital gains, and you are going to have to pay regular income tax on them.

However, there is one key difference in the case of a master limited partnership or MLP. In the case of a real estate trust, you are just considered an investor. However, in the case of a master limited partnership, you are considered to be a literal partner in the business. You are designated a limited partner, but you are a partner nonetheless, and so you can benefit from deducting the expenses that the company builds up. This is actually a big deal. These companies have a lot of depreciation of equipment, and so they pass that on to the partners. As a partner you are going to be able to deduct the depreciation that these companies pass on to you. So, although your income from these companies is going to be treated as regular income, you are probably only going to have to pay tax on 10-15% of the income that you earn from these companies. Many people that are heavily invested in these companies pay hardly any tax at all on the income that they earn from them.

So, what kind of companies are these? They are primarily energy companies. Specifically, they tend to be involved in oil and gas.

In the oil and gas industry, there are three ways that a company can be involved I the industry. These are classifications called upstream, midstream, and downstream. Upstream companies are involved in the actual drilling or fracking activities used to get the oil or gas.

Midstream companies are transport, storage, and sometimes refining companies. Finally, downstream companies actually sell the end products to consumers.

Of course, some large companies like Exxon are involved in all three areas.

Master limited partnerships are midstream companies. They may own oil pipelines. Or they may own storage tanks, including large storage tank facilities at ports. Or they might own trucks that are used to transport oil and natural gas. Other types of operations associated with master limited partnerships include rail terminals, refineries, and even oil tankers. Although there is a lot of talk about a so-called green economy, there is no sign that oil and gas are going away any time soon, and these types of businesses are probably going to be extremely reliable sources of income for investors for the foreseeable future and beyond.

The structure is similar to a real estate investment trust, in that there is a general partner who takes 10% of the money earned from the company as payment for managing it. Investors are paid 90% of the profits that the company earns.

Master limited partnerships are traded on the major stock exchanges. However, they are treated as partnerships for tax purposes. So, they work like a small business, in that they are a pass-through entity. As an investor, you are actually a partner in the company and so the income and expenses are passed through to you. This is not too complicated for taxes, the company will send you the appropriate forms with the information you need filled out, including the deductions that you are entitled to.

Like regular dividends from stocks, the profits from a master limited partnership that are passed through to the investors are paid out on a quarterly basis.

Typically, they pay very good dividends. As an example, consider Phillips 66 Partners LP. The stock trades at $52 a share. It pays an annual dividend of $3.42 a share, with a high yield of 6.6%.

One of the more famous MLPs is Magellan Midstream Partners. This company is involved in transportation and storage of refined petroleum products. It trades under the ticker MPLX LP. It pays an astounding yield of 9.76%. The share price is only $26.97, and the annualized payment is $2.67 per share.

Amerigas Partners LP is a company involved in the production and transport of propane natural gas. It is trading at $31 a share, and it pays an annual dividend of $3.80 a share. The yield on this security is 12.1%.

To get a better idea about this company, to use it as an example, it has 8,500 employees. It is annual revenue is around $3 billion. The company was founded in 1959.

As you can see, these types of companies have very high yields, often three or four times higher than what you would get with conventional stocks. Does that mean that you should sink all of your money into them? Of course, not – but it does offer a possibility to diversify your exposure in the markets to energy companies and take advantage of the income that they have to offer. There are many more choices than the ones that we have described here.

Not all MLPs are energy companies. There are some finance companies that have this type of organization, such as the Blackrock group. You can also invest in these on the stock exchanges.

Business Development Companies

There is a third class of company that you can invest in for dividend purposes that has a unique structure. These are financially oriented companies that are set up for the purpose of providing finance and investment capital in small to mid-sized businesses. Typically, they are going to invest in companies that are unable to get financing anywhere else, or they will seek out financially distressed companies that need a lifeline in order to survive. Often, they will invest in distressed companies and rebuild them to health. In other cases, they will act as venture capitalists, helping smaller companies that are not able to get money from investors like venture capitalists to get funding.

Business development companies also tend to pay relatively high dividend yields. In some cases, you might even benefit from capital appreciation. A BDC must invest 70% of it is capital, and like real estate investment trusts and master limited partnerships, they must pay out 90% of their profits to investors.

Business Development companies are a bit of a higher risk than master limited partnerships or real estate investment trusts. This is due to the nature of their business. They are providing capital to high risk small businesses, and so there are some risks that you as an investor are going to be exposing yourself to.

That said, the income potential is high. This is another example of the classic tradeoffs often faced in investing. That is, when there is higher risk involved, there is also often higher reward. In order to attract investors, a business development company pays high yields. They often range from 10-14%.

Business development companies bear some superficial resemblance to venture capital firms. However, there are many differences. A venture capital firm is only open to investment by extremely wealthy and well-connected individuals. Second, venture capital firms are primarily, if not exclusively, interested in breakthrough startup companies that are believed to have a good shot at ending up as a publicly traded company that has a high-profile IPO on the stock market.

Business development companies are open for investment to anyone who wants to buy shares in the company. They may invest in startups, but the focus is often on financially distressed companies that are unable to get financing through regular channels. So, the resemblance they have to venture capital firms, if you are seeing one, is actually pretty superficial. In many cases, if the distressed firm is beyond saving, they may break it up and sell off the assets in order to make a profit on their investment.

In addition to being high risk because these companies often provide funds to distressed companies – that might have a high risk of going under – business development companies are also sensitive to interest rate risk. Another downside to these companies, that may or may not be important depending on your situation, is that the income you earn from the dividends is treated as ordinary income. However, unlike a master limited partnership, you do not get any favorable tax treatment from pass through deductions.

Summary

Real estate investment trusts, master limited partnerships, and business development companies offer a unique opportunity to diversify your investments in unexpected ways.

You probably have not thought about investing in cell phone towers and companies that own oil tankers.

The high dividend payments coupled with relatively low share prices in most cases, will make these types of investments more accessible to those who are not able to come up with the cash needed in order to buy thousands of shares of IBM.

Therefore, it makes perfect sense to include some of these companies in your portfolio, if you feel like going this direction. Some investors will prefer sticking to standard investments in stocks like Apple, IBM, and Microsoft. However, you can gain wide exposure by investing in these types of companies. Just investing in REITs alone, you can invest in cell phone towers, nursing homes, cloud computing facilities, and rental homes. If you invested in master limited partnerships as well, you would be able to get exposure to large oil and gas operations that are likely to be evergreen streams of income. Then you can get finance into the mix by investing in one or more business development companies.

Having a truly diversified portfolio should be one of the most important goals when setting up your investment plan. Therefore, these types of companies are something to consider. The yields that are going to be available on most conventional energy companies are going to be far lower. Consider that Exxon Mobile has a yield of 4.91%. The share price is more than double that of Amerigas, and they offer the same payment per share, approximately. With a dividend payment of $3.50 a share, you would have to buy 2,857 shares of Exxon to earn $10,000 a year. This would require an initial investment of $197,133.

In order to get a $10,000 income from Amerigas, you would need 2,632 shares. The total investment required would be $81,579. This is a great educational illustration of the money you can save with an investment that has a higher yield. And this is something that must be strongly considered. And that is, conventional stocks are not going to be paying high yields like master limited partnerships unless there is something wrong with the stock. That is, you are going to find companies in trouble paying high yields, in order to keep attracting investors. The share price of the stock may have collapsed recently. In contrast, master limited partnerships pay high yields as a matter of course. These investments are far safer, and often offered by companies with good reputations that have been around for a long time. You should definitely consider adding some of these companies to your overall portfolio.

Chapter 8: Fundamental Analysis

The next topic that we are going to discuss is called fundamental analysis. This is an investigative activity that you are going to have to take on in order to fully understand the companies that you are investing in. It will take many phases if you are doing it thoroughly. It is an important step to use in order to determine the health and desirability of the companies that you invest in.

Choosing your companies

The first step in the investment process is to simply find the companies that you are the most interested in. Then from there, you can engage in a research process to determine which ones you will invest in after investigating their situation and which ones you are going to discard. The first step in this process is to look at the dividends that the company is paying.

Ask yourself these questions. Is the company showing a long history of paying increasing dividends? If not, why not? They had better have a good reason. Generally speaking, you are going to prefer companies that increase their dividend payment year after year. As we mentioned earlier, you want to make sure that they hold their dividend payments even during economic downturns.

Second, check the payout ratio to make sure that it is under 100%. If it is close to 50%, then this is a good sign.

If the dividend part of the equation checks out for your purposes, then you are ready to move on to the next state of the analysis.

Check P/E ratio

Next, you will want to check the P/E ratio. One thing that you want to stay away from is a stock that is overvalued. That might mean that at some point in the near future, the price of the stock is going to drop, to bring it back down to earth. You should compare the P/E ratio to similar companies, however. We mentioned this before in the context of looking for value stocks. In this context it does not matter if it is a value stock, you just want to make sure that the value is not way out of line one way or the other, particularly if it turns out to be really high. That could mean that there might be a price correction at some point in the future. That by itself may not be a deal killer, however.

Obtain Financial Reports

There are many financial reports that you can look at for a given company. The main ones you want to look at are the company prospectus and the 10-K. The 10-K is an audited financial statement that the company must file each year with the securities and exchange commission. You can get all the important information that you need about the financial health of the company from this report.

You are also going to want to read the prospectus, and any letters to the shareholders. Both will include very important information. This in fact, goes beyond mere financial statements. You are going to find information about the management team. This is going to include their current positions and their backgrounds. Also, you are going to want to read an analysis of the company's position in their market, which should be included in the prospectus. This should also include an analysis of the company's main competitors. It can be helpful to download the documents from the main competitors and see what they are saying in turn about your company, if they are saying anything at all.

What you want to look for is what markets the company is interested in penetrating in the future, and if they describe any plans for product releases or new services. You are going to want to evaluate the nature of the challenge provided by competitors and how the company is placed to deal with these problems.

Financial Statements

There are three main financial statements that you want to consider for fundamental analysis. These include the income statement, the balance sheet, and cash flow.

The income statement gives you basic information about the income the company brought in through total revenue. It will also provide gross profit, and information on important operating expenses that could indicate the future health of the company such as research and development spending. At the bottom of this statement, you are going to want to look at the net income of the company.

One thing that you are going to need to pay attention to are the trends that you see in these reports. Is the company showing better numbers in revenue and net income as the years go by? These are important things to look for as you do your analysis.

Next, you are going to want to go through the balance sheets of the company. This is where you are going to get information about assets and liabilities. For a dividend investor, one important thing to pay attention to is whether or not the company is taking on more debt. Remember that taking on debt is something that is going to mean having to make interest payments. Hate to say it, but in the hierarchy that exists, a dividend investor is below a creditor. That means if the company is taking on a lot of new debt and it is going to be required to make those interest payments, that means less money left over for dividends. In fact, going into debt can mean that the company will not be able to pay dividends in the future, or at the very least they are going to have to reduce them.

Other things to check on the balance sheet are trends in inventory and net receivables.

Finally, you are going to want to go over the cash flow statement for the company. This will include net income, expenses like depreciation, and investing activities like capital expenditure. Remember that investments in capital expenditure and research and development are important to pay attention to, these are things that indicate that the company is going to be healthy going forward.

The top Seven Factors

There are many things to consider when doing fundamental analysis that will help you decide whether or not a given company is a good investment or not. During your analysis there are a few things that you can look up quickly to get a feel for the company's current state of health. These items are things that are just on the company's stock market listing, so it is not necessary to go the prospectus or look up financial documents. They include:

- Earnings per share: This is the total profit earned by the company in a year divided by the current number of shares outstanding.

- Projected Earnings Growth (PEG): This is an estimate of the earnings growth rate over the coming year. Of course, it is a projection, and not a prediction, but it is important to look at.
- Price to earnings ratio: that is the price per share of the stock divided by the per share earnings. As we noted before, if it is unusually high and out of step with comparable companies, that might indicate future drops in share price.
- Price to sales ratio: This compares revenue of the company to share price. One thing to look for is how this matches up with price to earnings ratio. That is, how much is the company able to take out in profits.
- Price to book ratio: This is market value divided by book value. Book value is the value of assets that the company holds.
- Return on equity: this is the company's total net income divided by shareholder equity.
- Dividend payout ratio
- Dividend yield

Macro Considerations

Before looking at the specific company, you are going to want to look at the larger world in which the company finds itself. This is going to require that you take a look at the status of the economy at large. If the economy is not doing well, then you cannot put too much stock into the recent data from the company. Second, you should look at whether or not specific things going on in politics or the economy are impacting the company, such as new tariffs on an important input used in their products.

Then you want to look at the specific industry that the company is in. For example, if you were investing in Amerigas, you would want to look at the natural gas industry, to determine whether or not there were any events shaking up the industry that would have an impact on individual companies in the sector. From here, then you can begin to do the detailed analysis directly related to the company. This is going to involve looking at trends in earnings, profits, and estimates of future growth. Be sure to look for trends. You may want to look both annually, and by quarter. If you are looking at quarterly data, then you need to make sure to compare one quarter with the same quarter of the previous year.

Again, trends are important. You will want to do a quarterly analysis for the past year, and also annual analysis for the past three to five years. This will give you a very good picture of the health of the company and where it is going.

One thing to keep in mind is that every company is going to go through difficult times at some point. That does not mean the company is a bad investment, especially when we are considering investing in a company as a long-term project. If the company is facing difficulties at the present time, rather than just writing the company off, you might want to look into what the future prospects of the company are and what their plans are to turn things around. You might also want to look for management changes that have occurred or may occur, that could brighten the future prospects of the company. Another thing to consider is upcoming product releases, or new services that may be offered by the company that could mean increased growth in the coming years.

Fundamental analysis is not something you are going to restrict to corporate stocks. Remember that real estate investment trusts, master limited partnerships, and business development companies are businesses that also have the same financial statements that are publicly available. So, you are going to want to thoroughly investigate those companies as well before investing in them.

The next thing to look at is news about the company. Review any news coming out about the company on the various financial websites. Also review any straight news (that is non-financial) that may be coming out about the company. This could be news about government probes, or other things that could have a positive or negative impact on the company's prospects. For example, when Elizabeth Warren and people in Congress are talking about breaking up Amazon, that is not something that is going to bode well for Amazon if she ends up being elected as president.

When it comes to fund investing, you are going to want to do some analysis here as well. The first thing to look at is the performance of the fund. First, look up the year to date return. Then look up longer term performance metrics. See if the fund has had solid performance over five- and ten-year periods. You will want to see growth or at least some consistency in the annual returns. Then you need to compare yields and dividend payments.

The key thing that you are trying to do with fundamental analysis is determine whether the market is pricing the stock of the company at a fair market value. If the company looks solid, with increasing earnings and profits, but the market price of the stock is below the fair market value, then you have discovered a value stock that can be purchased at discount prices. If the stock is overpriced, then you might reconsider, or if the long-term prospects still look good, you might want to invest in the stock anyway.

Conclusion

Thank you for taking the time to read Dividend Investing: An easy guide for beginners to financial freedom in the stock market by making money using passive income. Simple investment strategies allowing you to quickly create wealth.

I hope that those of you who are beginners when it comes to the stock market have come away with a new found sense of knowledge about how the stock market works, what dividend payments are, and how you can use them to both grow wealth and to create a passive income stream.

Dividends remain one of the safest ways to grow income and wealth in the 21st century. The bottom line is that banks and investments in bonds no longer provide the type of income t hat people need any longer. This situation is not going to change any time soon, largely because of low interest rates. In fact, it is even getting worse. Recently the European Central Bank announced that it was cutting rates into the negative range. Imagine that, pretty soon you will have to pay the bank to keep your money there. The central bankers, of course, are hoping that people will go out and spend money and take on new debt. But the end result of all of this is that it only makes dividend stocks that much more attractive.

There is always investment risk present, you have the chance of losing all your money even when it is invested with the best companies around. However, if you invest in 10-20 solid companies that pay dividends, and you divide up these companies among different sectors and industries, you are probably going to be largely protected from large amounts of risk.

It may seem daunting, thinking about how you have to accumulate thousands of shares in order to make a good income from dividends. However, this is not really the case. You can build up the required number of shares by using a program of regular investing like clockwork, buying small numbers of shares at a time. So it is really not any different than saving money over a long time period in order to have a lot of it later. And you also benefit from the fact that we are talking about the stock market here. The flip side of risk is higher reward, and the appreciation in share value that is possible is something that will benefit investors.

We also talked about the possibility of using mutual funds or exchange traded funds in order to diversify your portfolio and as a different way to invest. Generally speaking, these funds pay lower yields, so may not be as attractive for cash income purposes because you will have to buy many more shares to get the same levels of income. However, since many of these funds have very high annual returns, they can provide a vehicle for those who are late investors to grow the amount of capital that they have available, very quickly. With returns hovering around 20%, this should not be too difficult.

No matter what you do, let me encourage all readers to take action, and start investing. Those that take action are going to be the ones who find themselves with wealth down the road.

Thanks again for taking the time to read this book. If you have found that the book was informative, please drop by Amazon.com and post a review for us. Thanks again!